# Stop Hoping...
# Start Hunting!

## JENNIFER K. HILL

Copyright ©2013 JHill Publishing

ISBN: 978-0-578-1085-5-1

Library of Congress Control Number: 2013907973

Printed in the United States of America.

# Dedication

For my husband, Ian, who has always believed in and encouraged me. Also, my family, who taught me from a young age that I could always be whatever I dreamed of and that if I worked hard, no goal was ever unattainable.

# Table of Contents

# Preface

It is one week before Thanksgiving and I am referred a new job seeker, Sue, who was recently laid off. We meet for coffee on a crisp morning in downtown Los Angeles at Starbucks to discuss her job search. She begins by lamenting how she has never been laid off or let go in her life and does not know what to do. Additionally, she expresses her concerns about not being able to find a job over the holidays and relays that she does not know what to do, as she is the primary breadwinner in her family.

Does this story sound familiar? It is a story that many a job seeker I have met with has faced. I see it all too often when an intelligent, capable employee is laid off or let go for some reason or another and the situation proceeds to break their bank and their spirit. When someone is laid off around the holidays, it can be even more challenging for that job seeker.

So how is this story any different than all the others out there about unemployed job seekers who are despondent and do not see any access to having their old career or any career back? This story is about perspective. It is about how one's perspective can shift the way a circumstance occurs and, in turn, shift the outcome of that person's future.

That day, I sat there and listened empathetically to the story I had heard all too many times before, but on this day, I decided to offer some coaching that I do not always offer. I asked Sue how that perspective was working out for her.

She replied, "What perspective?"

"The perspective that your circumstances are outside of your control and that your holidays are going to be miserable. That you are bad and/or wrong for having been laid off and that you will never find another job or at least not as good or well-paying of a job," I responded.

She laughed nervously, and then took a moment to think about. "I guess it kind of sucks."

"Yes," I concurred, "it does, doesn't it?" I continued on, "Are you open to looking at this situation from a different perspective that could give you access to having one of the best holidays of your life?"

She looked at me incredulously but answered with a slight enthusiasm, "Absolutely!"

I went on to discuss with her how her thoughts and her words were going to create exactly what she feared most: no job and no money for her family. The only thing we have in life is our thoughts and what we say about them (i.e., our perspective). In her case, she was saying what many unemployed people say: "It's hard," "I won't find a job," "I cannot find a job," "I am not as young as I used to be," etc.

What happens when we use this language and think these disempowering thoughts, I explained, is that we begin to create that disempowering reality as the truth. Most people sit around hoping for a miracle or some even go out and aggressively look for a job "hoping" that something good will turn out for them, but the language they use and the thoughts they think are counterproductive to their intended outcome: getting a job.

"So what do I do?" she asked. Well, that is the question, isn't it? What can you do to alter the way you think, act and speak so that your thoughts and words align with your intention?

"What would it be like," I asked, "if you shifted your perspective and saw this as an opportunity rather than an obstacle?"

"I am not sure I understand," she replied, confused.

"When was the last time you had a month or more off around the holidays with your husband and children where you got to enjoy every moment with them?"

"I cannot remember," she said.

"What if you were to look at this layoff as a gift? A chance to spend a month off with your family and to cherish every moment you have with them and know without a shadow of a doubt that you will have an even better job come the New Year?"

"That would be a miracle!" She exclaimed. "How would I possibly do that?"

We sat down and went through what I am going to teach you in this book, which is to take HOPE out of the job hunt and put together an intentional action plan, including a Statement of Intent and a Daily Declaration. Yes, in this book you will also learn about how to effectively job hunt and interview, but this is not just a how-to book on being effective at job hunting. This is a book about the mental AND physical work that it takes to shift your perspective around your job hunt and give yourself access to the career you have always wanted.

That day, we created a Statement of Intent and a Daily Declaration for Sue. We will discuss what these methods are in later chapters. By the time we completed our interview, she had access to a new perspective on her job search and a new action plan on how to be effective in achieving her goals.

A few weeks later, I received a call on Christmas Eve. It was Sue. She was in tears. At first, I was worried that something had happened, but through her tears she managed to get out "Jennifer, I want you to know that these are not tears of sadness; rather, they are tears of joy. Thanks to your coaching and feedback I have had the most amazing last few weeks celebrating the holidays with my family, and that would not have been possible if you had not helped me shift my perspective. I also want you to know that I have not found a job yet, but it does not even concern me. I have been doing my Daily Declaration and focusing on my Statement of Intent every day and there is not a question in my mind that I will have a job come the New Year. Thank you for what you taught me."

Less than two weeks later, I got a call a few days after the New Year and it was Sue. "Jennifer, I want you to know that I got a job, and not only that, it is closer to home and pays me more money. Thank you for what you taught me. I will always remember you."

This story is an example of what you can learn from the lessons in this book. You can learn how to stop hoping and start hunting. You can learn how to proactively go after and get what you want not only in the job hunt, but also in many areas of your life where you are willing to shift your perspective and take action.

My commitment is that you will choose to take the hope out of your job hunt by the time you finish this book.

# Introduction

*"Don't ask what the world needs. Ask what makes you come alive, and go do it. Because what the world needs is people who have come alive."*

*Howard Thurman*

THE ECONOMY HAS NOT BEEN GREAT IN THE LAST FEW YEARS. WE ALL know it. We have just had a recession, and we are just emerging out of it and into what people are calling the "jobless recovery." That means that a lot of us are looking for work, and that a lot of people who have found work are underemployed, or feel stuck doing jobs that they do not enjoy while their skills are not being used to their fullest potential.

There are a lot of reasons for looking for work—whether you are a recent grad, looking to change career paths, or have been laid off. But everyone has basically the same goals. We all want success—both materially and figuratively. We want to be fulfilled by the work we do and we want to be rewarded for it.

Amid all the bad news you might be hearing, the good news is that for anyone who applies the right principles this goal is possible! Know what you want, follow your dream and know how to deal with the challenges ahead, and you can be paid very well to do what fulfills you as an individual. I know the tricks for making this happen, and I am excited about sharing them with you.

## WHO AM I?

By profession, I am a recruiter, which means, in short, that it is my job to work for companies to find the best candidates to fill their positions.

In a way, I am an employment matchmaker. I work closely with companies and with candidates, so I know what each end of this equation wants from the other. This means I know exactly what companies are looking for from you when they evaluate whether you would be the right fit for a position.

So how did I get here?

Personally, I was bored to tears in high school. I graduated with a GED when I was sixteen so that I could study for a degree. What for most people would have been their last two years of high school I spent at junior college. I moved on to the University of California Irvine for the second two years of my bachelor's degree and planned to move on to law school.

I graduated in June, and moved to Los Angeles. Everything was going according to plan—until in September I got a call from my college saying that I had not actually graduated. I had missed a class from high school. I did not have U.S. History 101, and it did not matter that I had taken Advanced Placement European History instead in high school and passed it. Sound like any institutions you have ever dealt with?

It seemed like the worst thing that had happened in my entire life. But now I know that it ended up being the best thing.

The college's solution was to send me a thousand-page U.S. History 101 textbook to read and memorize for a two-hour exam with the Dean of Social Sciences less than a month later. The extra studying was nothing. What it really meant for me was that I could not go to law school that year.

I took the test and passed with flying colors—but now I had a year in front of me that I had no idea what to do with. My dream of law school had to be placed on hold—and that is one of the most frustrating feelings in the world.

I ended up posting my resume on monster.com and got a call from a recruiting agency, who wanted to recruit me for a sales job. They brought me in and introduced me to the thought of being a recruiter (at the time I did not even know what being a recruiter was!)—and almost in spite of myself I ended up getting a job as a recruiter with them.

I worked this entry-level recruiter job for about four months, learned the tricks and seized my opportunity. The company I was working for recruited for other agencies, so when an order came in from one of our job owners—$50,000–$75,000 per year to a recent grad with some experience—to me, this was a dream job. So I took a risk and reached out personally to the employer. I essentially called the president of the company on his direct line and convinced him that he was going to hire me and that I was going to be the best thing that ever happened to his firm. It took a lot of guts, but it paid off—and I ended up being the youngest, most successful person they had ever hired.

In short, I took what could have been a setback, acted courageously to go for what I wanted and presented myself in the most useful possible light to my potential employer. These are all essential tools in finding your ideal career. As you can tell from the story, they have been very good to me. Over the years as a recruiter I have seen them be very good to others as well, and I think it is time to share what I have learned with all of you.

The biggest lesson I have learned is that passion and skills are an unstoppable combination. My goal with this book is to help teach you the skills and release the passion you already have that will lead you to true success—a good job doing what you love.

# 1 | Should You Make a Move and/or Change Jobs?

*"Build your own dreams, or someone else will hire you to build theirs."*

*Farrah Gray*

## THE FISH BOWL—WHO NEEDS SUCCESS?

I recently was having coffee with a friend where we were discussing the state of the economy and my work on this book. I was explaining how my rationale behind writing the book was to inspire people to achieve their dreams and find something they are passionate about that pays them well. During this conversation, my friend raised an interesting question: "What if some people simply have no desire do to be successful?"

I have to admit, I was rather dumbfounded by this. I asked her to elaborate, as this was a foreign concept to me. Doesn't everyone want to be successful in his or her own right? Her response was one that caused me to pause and think. She explained that we all live in a fish bowl; however, because the fish bowl is glass, and therefore transparent, it is almost impossible to see the fish bowl that you are in. She shared with me a cathartic moment she had experienced, where she was able to see herself from outside the fish bowl. What does this mean? It means that, from her perspective, most of us go through our day-to-day lives swimming about in our fish bowl, unaware that there is anything available outside of what we can conceive. A certain few, though, realize the limitations the fish bowl imposes upon them, and they choose to live a life outside of the fish bowl, where things are less certain, but anything is possible.

People who choose to live outside the fish bowl can still see into it; however, they embrace the uncertainty and the unease that comes from living on the outside. A wise person once said, "If you are not expanding, then you are contracting." The same could be said for the people who choose to free themselves of their constraints. They are fearless in the face of the unknown; and in being unstoppable, they often achieve their dreams.

The important point about the fish bowl is that those who are in the fish bowl and are content to be in the fish bowl should not be forced to live a life outside of the fish bowl, outside of their comfort zone. If someone chooses to spend their life or career swimming in the fish bowl, with no ambition to ever attain success or even possible failure by leaving their comfort zone, those outside of the fish bowl should NEVER force anyone to embrace the alternative option.

Look at your life. Are you content to simply "go with the flow" and live a life where you might not ever achieve your dreams, but you might have a great life? If living a simple life works for you, then there is no need to change. If instead you are someone who wants everything that life has to offer, and are not afraid of possible failure, then embrace your fears in working towards success. Acknowledge that you have spent your entire life being comfortable, but if you are truly committed, you can choose to leave the fish bowl and carve out your own path. Failure may come, often more than once, but if you persevere the rewards on the other side of the glass will be plentiful.

My benefit is to offer people tools to set measurable goals, minimize fear and achieve their dreams.

Think about this when you think about whether you are satisfied with what you have or if you want to reach to achieve something more. Dare to dream as big as you can when you think about your future career, because my idea with this book is to give you the tools to make that dream a reality.

## DANGER OR OPPORTUNITY?

Everybody has his or her own reasons for looking for a new job. Maybe you have been laid off. This is not something anybody looks forward to, but does being laid off place you in danger or present you with a new opportunity?

I would assert that whether you see a layoff as an opportunity or not is all in your point of view. Many people mistakenly equate being laid off with being fired. When you are fired that means a company has terminated you based on performance or some other element related to your work. However, being laid off simply means that there has been some sort of reduction in force or perhaps a change in the structure of the company.

If you can alter your perspective on having been laid off, then you can begin to see a layoff as an opportunity rather than a danger or something "bad" that happened to you.

The following are three ways that you could begin to look at a layoff as an opportunity.

1. Change in career. You can embrace your layoff as a chance to pursue the career you have always wanted, perhaps even open up your own business. Job seekers often spend years or even decades in a career that is unsatisfying. Being laid off can give you the chance to re-invent yourself and what you are committed to. You can finally pursue what you are passionate about if you have not been doing so already.

2. Increase in salary. Recently I interviewed a high-level executive who shared with me his story of how he was laid off in his prior position. At the time of the layoff he initially felt frustrated, as many people do. However, in the long run, he was extremely grateful for the up-ward mobility and the increase in pay the layoff afforded him. It was unlikely that he would have left the comfort of his old job had he not been laid off. He would have probably spent the next ten years trying to achieve the same level in his career and increase in salary that he accomplished in less than twelve months in a new position!

3. Move up the ladder. After being in a job for many years you can begin to plateau. Sometimes you need a little fire to jump-start your ambition and drive. By being laid off, you can reevaluate where you want to be in your current career. By doing this, you can shift your energies and focus to pursuing a promotion that you had long forgotten you desired. A new company means new bosses, a new environment, a new set of tasks to learn and opportunity for growth.

Opportunities can often come in different shapes and sizes. Sometimes an opportunity might even be disguised as a layoff. It is up to you to recognize an opportunity for what it is and to always be open to the possibilities that are available to you.

If you have been laid off, do not miss the opportunity to turn a potential disappointment into a real opportunity. If there was something you were dissatisfied with about your old job, take this chance to grasp the real success you have always wanted!

## CAN I AFFORD TO CHANGE CAREERS?

With thousands of people being laid off every month many people are beginning to reconsider what they want to do with the rest of their lives. Do they work tirelessly to try and get some version of their old job back? Do they transition into a new growing field that offers more opportunity than their old profession or do they go after their long lost dream? How do you know if a career change is right for you—and if it is the right choice, what do you do next?

The first thing you have to ask yourself is, on a scale of 1–10, how much did you love your old job? If you rate your old job as a 7 or lower, then it might be time to consider pursuing a different field. In this economic climate it is not worth your time to spend ten times the amount of effort to get the same job back that you were not crazy about to begin with. Rather, you are better off investing your time and energy into finding something you love. Some of you may already have hobbies and interests that you could see yourself turning into a career. Others might need to evaluate your strengths and weaknesses and find something that would suit you long term.

If you do decide that changing careers is the right move for you, then there are a few steps you should take to begin the process. First, discover WHAT you want to do.

If you know that you do not want to go back to your old field, but are confused as to what you might want to do, then finding yourself a career coach is probably the next logical step. It is always a good idea to get a referral when trying to find a career coach rather than trying to find one on your own. There are also various career assessment tests that you can take to help you reevaluate in what direction you should take your career. One example of a career assessment test that you could take is the Jung Career Indicator: www.humanmetrics.com/cgi-win/JTypes2.asp.

Regardless of what you choose, know that there are options available to you other than just going back to the same boring job you hate. Look at your layoff as an opportunity to re-create yourself and your future.

## SHOULD I BE GRATEFUL FOR A JOB I DO NOT LIKE?

> *"Holding on to anger is like drinking poison and expecting the other person to die."*
>
> *Buddha*

How important is it to be grateful for a job, even if you do not like it? Very! I have news for those of you out there who are ungrateful for your job—your boss knows it and eventually it can come back to bite you in the butt! Being both a recruiter and a career coach, I speak with thousands of job seekers every year and hundreds of employers. It is interesting to hear what both employers and employees have to say given the current market conditions.

There are a lot of ungrateful and fed up employees and employers out there. Many of the job seekers I talk to feel underappreciated and taken advantage of in this economy. Often, they may feel like an extra burden has been put on them, and that they are being undercompensated for the extra work they are performing. On the flip side, a lot of employers feel that their employees are taking it for granted that they have a paying job and benefits in this tough economy. So what does this mean for everyone?

Some people may choose to make a change because they truly are dissatisfied and there is nothing their employer can do to change their situation, but others can avoid having to go through the difficulty of finding something new simply by putting on their gratitude-colored glasses. So what are gratitude glasses and how can you put them on? Everyone has heard the term "rose-colored glasses" and knows that means seeing the world through a "rosy" point of view. There is a fascinating concept I heard of years ago, which is that you can choose a different perspective or set of glasses every day to come from which can empower you. One example of this is gratitude. When I say that you can put on a pair of "gratitude-colored glasses," this simply means to choose to come from a perspective of gratitude for that day or that week or that month.

When you choose to put on your gratitude-colored glasses, you are then choosing to see everything that happens to you through the lens of gratitude. Even if you get blown off by your boss or get in an argument with someone at the office, you find a way to be grateful for that fight or that upset and learn from it. If both employers and employees could learn to do this, there would be a lot less movement in people's jobs and a lot more happiness for everyone in the workplace in general. Next time your boss is frustrated with you, try to find a way to learn something from that situation and be grateful for what you learn.

I share with you a wonderful quote from a friend of mine who was looking for a job. I had told him about the "gratitude-colored glasses" theory I had heard about and he emailed me the following:

Subject: My Gratitude Glasses – Thought You Would Appreciate This

*"Gratitude unlocks the fullness of life. It turns what we have into enough, and more. It turns denial into acceptance, chaos into order, confusion into clarity.... It turns problems into gifts, failures into success, the unexpected into perfect timing, and mistakes into important events. Gratitude makes sense of our past, brings peace for today and creates a vision for tomorrow."*

~ Melodie Beattie

## SO HOW CAN I BE SURE WHEN IT IS TIME TO CHANGE JOBS?

Maybe you are caught between gratitude for your current position and the itch to try something new. What do you need to know if you are looking to make a move? Consider this: There is more competition than ever before. In 2010 the people who were employed were just trying to keep their jobs, but now they feel underpaid and undervalued and are willing to fight for what they are worth. This said, it is more important than ever to prepare even more thoroughly before your next interview. Get a coach or ask a friend to go through the typical interview questions with you. If you know a recruiter, ask for tutorials to brush up your skills.

There is finally room to negotiate again. A couple of years ago, whatever jobs were available were simply out of necessity and therefore the money just was not there. This year, employers are actually considering adding additional talent. It is because of this that there finally will be more money on the table. For the first time in several years I am beginning to see people get offers for what they are really worth (not quite as good as 2005–2007, but definitely better!).

## HAVE YOU *CHOSEN* YOUR CAREER?

*"Nothing is really work unless you would rather be doing something else."*
*James Barrie (creator of Peter Pan)*

Is your current job or career path something you are passionate about? If not, then know that you are not alone. A large number of people go their whole lives doing something they are not inspired by, yet they do it all the same because they figure it is the best that they can get. This sort of apathetic view of life and of one's career is very comfortable for a lot of people, and as human beings, we like to be comfortable. The reason that many people never try to change careers is because they are scared of the unknown. They are terrified of moving out of their comfort zone. On the one hand, you have a job that you know you can perform adequately, and be paid a fair enough sum for, but on the flip side you live your life always wondering what could have been if perhaps you had pursued a different path.

Have you ever found yourself wondering what life would have been like if you had not chosen the career path that you are on? If instead of going to law school, you had chosen to take an art class or become a teacher? What would your life look like? Would that be a life that you find fulfilling and that you would be excited to get out bed every day and do it?

How many of us hear our alarm go off at 6 a.m. and dread getting up to go to work? How many hours and days of your life are you willing to waste hating your job and complaining about how unfair it is that you are not paid more or treated better? Would you like to know a secret of people who are successful?

They are not willing to settle just for the sake of being comfortable! When their alarm goes off at 6 a.m. they are typically excited to get out of bed, and cannot wait to start another day doing something they love. What would life be like for you if you were exhilarated every day by the work that you did and the contribution that you made to others? Wouldn't it be a life worth living if you got to wake up every day and do something you loved? Making money and being successful in your chosen field does take work. It takes a lot of dedication and perseverance to achieve long-term success, but once you have, you will never want to go back.

Let's take a look at the story of somebody who made a strong choice about where he wanted to go, and following it passionately became one of his greatest decisions.

## CAPTURING THE MOMENT: CHASE'S STORY

I would like to share a story with you from a world famous photographer who I interviewed for this book several years ago at the Sundance Film Festival. His name is Chase Jarvis, and his story is one you will not soon forget.

Chase grew up as an only child, and he knew from a very early age that he wanted to express his creativity in the world in some way. Like many of us, Chase stifled his creativity in exchange for promises of financial security and stability. Chase was offered a soccer scholarship to one of the best schools in the country, and thought that being a professional soccer player would offer him what was missing from his life. He was an extremely talented soccer player, and continued to play through some of his college years. However, he quickly began to realize that being a professional athlete was not really his dream.

He instead thought he wanted riches and a career that he could count on. He began to pursue a medical degree, studying the sciences and focusing his energy on becoming a doctor. Yet something was still missing. Being a doctor did not make sense either. He finally decided to major in Philosophy, and when he graduated from college he began pursuing a PhD in the subject. All the while, his parents supported him in whatever choices he made. They continued to support their son through his various endeavors in a variety of fields.

Shortly after he began pursuing his PhD, he had an epiphany. After a five-month trip backpacking through Europe, and much introspection and self-evaluation, he realized that he was meant to be an artist—specifically a photographer. Chase knew it would be a long and arduous journey ahead if he decided to forgo his prior education and pursue an entirely new field, but this did not stop him. He pushed ahead into unknown territories.

He committed himself entirely to becoming successful in his chosen field of photography. He worked tirelessly, learning everything he needed to know about photography by experience rather than education. He pushed himself to new limits, sometimes working upwards of 80–100 hours a week when necessary. He knew he was destined to be a great photographer and would stop at nothing to achieve his dream. From the very beginning he was confronted with his own demons, as well as the peer pressure from society and his friends to do something more traditional. He knew full well that being an independent artist he would have to work exceptionally hard to make the same kind of money that he could have made had he become a doctor.

Despite the lack of any formal education in his chosen field, and the thousands of "nos" he initially received, he persevered. He pushed himself to new limits, and never stopped believing that he could achieve his dream. Only a few years into his career he became wildly successful. The same people who had once told him "no" were now lining up to hire him as a professional photographer. Chase never let himself get sidetracked by fear or doubt, and he attributes much of his success to his positive mental attitude. He explained that creative artists are confronted with a lot more negativity compared with many other professions.

He saw the down economy as a perfect chance to grow his business because he knew in his core that what he was doing was right for him. In September 2009 he launched an iPhone app called "Best Camera" that has been rated one of the top twenty apps by magazines such as *NY Magazine* and *Wired*. From the beginning he was a pioneer in his field who was never afraid to be transparent and to push the boundaries of what was acceptable in the world of photography. He was one of the first photographers to take his audience behind the scenes on a photo shoot, and he now has the largest following of any independent photographer in the world (He has approximately 2,000,000 followers on his blog, which can be found at http://blog.chasejarvis.com/blog/).

When asked what piece of advice he would give to someone who aspired to the level of success that he has achieved he shared: "Follow your passion. Do not think for a second that your passion cannot get you six figures or even seven figures. If you are passionate about crocheting, then crochet. Start a crochet blog. It has never been easier to make a career out of something you are passionate about."

I think that Chase's story is something we can all learn from. Many of us sell out for money or comfort, but at the end of the day, you have to love what you do otherwise you will live your life wondering what could have been if you had followed your dreams.

# 2 | **Finding the Job**

*"Failure & set-backs are necessary components to life-shattering success."*

*Unknown*

## WHERE DO I EVEN BEGIN?

If you are new to the workforce, or if you have been in the same position for many years, you may be lost as to where you should even start in looking for a job. Do not worry. Not knowing how or where to look for a job is one of the biggest obstacles most job seekers face in their job search, but by reading this book and dedicating yourself to your job hunt, you have taken the most important step. So where do you begin?

The following is an overview of the top six things that you should do to get started with your job search.

1. Create a Wishlist of exactly what you are looking for in your next position. It is important to know what you want and what you are willing to accept so that when the right opportunity arises you will be able to recognize it. A Wishlist might contain such items as "Salary," "Benefits," "Environment," "Location," "Company Culture," "Hours," "Title," etc. In addition to creating a Wishlist with the specifics of what you want, it is also important to assign a percentage to each item on your Wishlist. Once you have done so, all of your Wishlist items should total 100%. From there, you will need to have an honest conversation with yourself about what percentage of your overall Wishlist you are willing to accept. Do you need 60%, 75% or 90% of your overall Wishlist in order to accept a new position? Once you figure this out, you can then go through each job opportunity as it arises and see how it meets your Wishlist criteria, and whether it is a good idea to move forward with that particular opportunity.

   **SAMPLE WISHLIST**

   - 100k+ total compensation package = 30%
   - Within fifteen miles of home = 15%
   - Company with over 100 employees = 5%
   - Ability to work from home as needed = 10%
   - Vacation time of three weeks or more per year = 10%
   - Director level or higher title = 10%

- 401k contribution = 5%
- Opportunity for bonus = 5%
- Medical benefits = 5%
- Reimbursed tuition = 2.5%
- Fast-paced environment = 2.5%

2. Write a great resume that effectively presents the value you have to offer a company. I am not a huge fan of posting your resume on www.monster.com or www.careerbuilder.com, but that is up to you. Keep reading and I will share my tips for writing a resume that knocks their socks off.

3. Go to www.indeed.com and set yourself up with email alerts for different positions in your area (more on this later).

4. Use the 30/30/30 rule (see the next section for more details).

5. Find a recruiter. If you are someone who specializes in a particular field, having a recruiter can be a great resource for you. You may want to meet with three or four recruiters to choose efficiently who you want to represent you. It is perfectly acceptable to have more than one recruiter working with you; however, it is important that you keep meticulous track of where you resume has been sent.

6. Brush up on your interviewing skills. Getting the interview is half the battle. The other half is not talking yourself out of the position. Find a career coach or a friend who can help you prepare for your interviews. There is more to come on networking and interviews— they are two of the most important areas as to whether you land the job, and I have learned a lot over the years that will help you out.

This may seem daunting at first, but if you take it one step at a time you will be landing your dream job in no time. Reading this book is a great first step. Stick with me and I will help you through the details!

## MAXIMIZE YOUR TIME—THE 30/30/30 RULE

What is the 30/30/30 rule and how can you use it to find your next job? The 30/30/30 rule is something I have come up with to help guide job seekers on how to effectively maximize their time during their job search. We all know that times are tough and it is not as easy as it used to be to get an interview, let alone a job offer. It is for this reason that the 30/30/30 rule is a perfect guideline to help you understand what you should be doing to get yourself interviews and job offers.

For the 30/30/30 rule, I recommend that you spend 30% of your time attending networking events during your job search, 30% of your time using social media tools such as LinkedIn, Twitter and Facebook to help you find a job and 30% of your time applying to positions online. If the 30/30/30 rule has been utilized effectively the last 10% of your time will be spent out on interviews.

Why spend 30% of your time networking? The reason is simple. Over 80% of positions are found through word of mouth, and for the 80% of people who find jobs via word of mouth the majority of jobs are found through casual acquaintances, such as the people you meet at networking events.

Why spend 30% of your time using social media? Job hunting is a whole new ball game with websites like Twitter and LinkedIn now advertising jobs. You can both passively and actively job hunt through these websites.

Finally, you should be spending 30% of your time applying for jobs. This is a no-brainer, but bears mentioning. I often have candidates come into my office and tell me that they cannot find anything. When I ask them how many places they have applied to they often give me a blank stare. You cannot find a job if you are not at least sending out your resume. Send your resume to companies that have positions posted, but do not be afraid to reach out to companies that might not be actively looking.

## 30% NETWORKING

In the world of job seeking, nothing rings truer than the adage "It is not what you know; it is who you know." Listing your qualifications on a resume and then sending it out blindly en masse may be easy, but without a personal connection, you are just words on a page, and your qualifications will not get more than a glance.

It pays to be upfront about it when getting to know people for business purposes—after all, they know it may very well pay to know *you* at some point—and because of its importance there are countless ways to do it. Regardless of what type of job you might be looking for, one thing is certain: The better you are at networking the more easily you will land your next position!

## Keys to networking

How does one become an effective networker? The good news is that it is not something you have to be born with; it is something you can learn. I remember one of the first networking events I went to when I launched my own company, wherein I did not have a clue! I accosted every person I encountered by forcing my business card upon them and then chatting their ear off for at least ten minutes at a time. (If you were one of the people at that event at Wokano, I apologize!)

Networking is an art form. You have to learn what is effective and what is not in order to be effective in a networking situation. To be effective at networking there are a few things you must do. The following is a list of points that can increase your effectiveness in a networking situation.

1. Have an enticing "hook." This is critical not only in job hunting, but in business in general. You want to be the one person that is remembered at the end of the day. It is important to capture your audience's attention and avoid overwhelming them with so much information that their eyes glaze over.

2. Keep it short and sweet. Try not to talk to one person for more than five minutes at a time. You can always follow up with someone for a coffee after the event, but keep in mind it is unlikely you will get the chance to network with all of those same people again.

3. Always have a firm handshake and good eye contact! Having a firm handshake and good eye contact indicates confidence. Confidence is something that people find attractive, and more important, *memorable*. Networking is all about being memorable at the end of the day. Someone who has a weak handshake, or does not have strong

eye contact, is easily forgotten. If you are nervous about making eye contact, practice looking yourself in the eye in the mirror while you give your Elevator Speech, or ask a friend to "role play" with you.

4. Get to know people and ask what you can do for them. No one likes a person who is all about ME, ME, ME. Unfortunately, many people have turned networking events into nothing more than being a walking, talking billboard. People will often walk up and hand you their card before you know anything about them. This is not what networking is about. It is about creating long-lasting, sustainable and trustworthy relationships. Next time you are in a networking situation, wait for the person you are speaking with to ask for your card or ask them for their card. When someone takes the time to ask for your card, they will be much more likely to remember who you are.

5. Follow up! If you do not follow up with the people you meet, you are simply wasting your time. I find that people who attend networking events are often confused as to what they are supposed to do after the event is over. The answer is simple: Follow up! What does following up mean? It means taking the time to send a follow-up email the next day. If you can make the email personal, it will be more meaningful. In your follow-up, you might want to offer a potential referral or resource, or mention a subject that was discussed at the networking event.

Remember: It is not about you; it is about them! People will go out of their way to connect with you and help you if you pay it forward by helping them!

## Learn Chinese—*Guanxi*

I recently had the opportunity to pick the brain of a very successful, high-level manager with an entertainment company in Paris. His name is Guillaume. Guillaume has been with his organization for close to ten years. However, during his tenure with the company, he took fifteen months off to travel to China and learn Chinese, as well as to learn more about the Chinese culture. He gained many insights during this process, but one of the most important things he learned about was *guanxi*.

*Guanxi* describes a personal connection between two people in which one is able to prevail upon another to perform a favor or service, or be prevailed upon. We have a word for this in English as well. We call it networking.

*Guanxi* is a central concept in Chinese society that is ingrained into the culture. *Guanxi* is used to develop and maintain strong client relationships and a competitive edge over the competition in business; however, the same business principles of *guanxi* can also be applied to looking for a job.

Having the support of a strong network can exponentially increase your effectiveness in both job hunting and in business. Building a network does not mean simply meeting people just to help you with a specific situation such as looking for a job. Building a network is a life-long endeavor that will create a foundation for long-term success and opportunities.

You will not be able to have sustainable success, however, if you do not have trust within the network (this also applies to your social media networks!). According to Guillaume, to create trust in both business and job-hunting situations, you must be transparent and sincere with the people in your network. It becomes clear very quickly if you are only out for personal gain. If instead you create a symbiotic network, one that is reciprocal, you will readily create the results you desire.

Always remember that, while you may be able to have short-term success on your own, long-term success cannot be sustained alone. *Guanxi* is your source of the knowledge and resources that will create your personal success!

## Mixing and mingling

What do job seekers who get hired have in common? They do not sit around and wait for someone to hire them! Rather than waiting for the perfect opportunity to fall into their lap, they go out and network with people who can help them land their next position.

How do you know what events to attend or where to meet people? There are a variety of events that you can attend which can help you land your next job. In some cases, you might want to go to specific job hunter meetings such as Pink Slip Mixers or Challenger Group meetings.

In other situations, you might want to attend business mixers such as Chamber of Commerce meetings or various gatherings related to your industry. If you are looking for an informal way to get together with people who have similar interests to you then you might want to check out Meetup Groups (www.meetup.com). For a full list of networking opportunities in your area, check out an online resource such as http://inthecalendar.com/.

Regardless of where you go to network, the idea is to get yourself out there and start connecting. I recommend attending at least one networking event a week if you are unemployed, or at least two a month if you are currently working.

Remember, mixing is an important tactic, since 80% of jobs are filled through word of mouth!

## Keep your eyes open

Some time ago I attended a Pink Slip Mixer in Westwood. Towards the end of the night, a job seeker who I had been coaching came up to me and we began to catch up. When I asked him how his job search was coming, he replied "Great!" and shared with me that he had just met a fantastic lead at the bar who had given him three phone numbers of potential leads that might be interested in hiring him! The person he met was not even someone that was part of our group. Rather, this job seeker was at the bar and began chatting with the man next to him. During this conversation, he quickly learned that this man was recently divorced and had just moved to the area from New York (this job seeker's home state). He immediately started to chat with him and offer him resources on great places to meet people in Los Angeles. The fact that the job seeker started to offer resources first is critical. By offering to help someone else, they will be more inclined to help you in return.

After a short conversation with the gentleman at the bar, the job seeker mentioned he was in the digital media field, and sure enough, the man he was talking to wound up being a senior vice president for a huge cable channel. The man immediately wrote down three phone numbers for the job seeker to call the next day, and even recommended that the job seeker use his name.

Stories like this are the very reason that you should always treat every person as a potential lead. You never know where your next job lead can come from. It could even be from the guy next to you at the bar.

## Increase your net worth by increasing your network

Larry Benet, the most well-networked man on the planet, once told me that "Your Network = Your Net Worth." Owning a staffing firm, I have found this to be very accurate. A lot of job seekers undervalue the resources that are right under their noses, primarily their social media accounts such as LinkedIn, Twitter and Facebook.

No matter who you are, or what your employment status is, chances are that you will occasionally get the chance to attend a party or two. It is important to get a business card from each person you meet at a party. I always recommend connecting with an individual within 24 hours after meeting them at a party via one of your primary social media accounts. This shows enthusiasm and good follow-up skills. Additionally, quick follow-up makes you more memorable. So remember, the next time you are a party, have a goal of getting at least three or more business cards and following up with those individuals via social media within 24 hours. Your social media accounts will keep you connected to them, and there is no telling what good may come of it.

## 30% SOCIAL MEDIA

### LinkedIn

You probably already have a Facebook page. Maybe you have a Twitter account too. Chances are that you had a MySpace back when it was big. Can there really be a reason for you to bother with yet another social network? The answer is a definite YES! LinkedIn, if you are not already familiar with it, is a social network for professionals. Its stated goal is to bring the world of in-person business networking online and worldwide—and this could have a huge impact for you.

LinkedIn is especially useful for people who are recent graduates— a demographic that has recently been struggling to find adequate and appropriate employment.

People on LinkedIn know that what goes around comes around, and they are there to do only two things: to find work for themselves and to help other people (you, for instance!) find work. Still not convinced?

### The top five reasons to be on LinkedIn

1. Create a virtual resume. You can post a virtual resume, which can be viewed by recruiters and hiring managers who are looking to hire.

2. Research. You can use LinkedIn to research a company you are interested in working at, and find out if you know anyone that can get you in the door. The more people you are connected to, the more companies and people you will be able to view. Another way to research using LinkedIn is to research the person you are meeting with prior to your interview.

3. Networking. Many people are unsure what to do once they have met with someone at a networking event. LinkedIn makes it easier than ever to connect with that person immediately after your networking event. You can then use their name as a future resource for potential job connections. LinkedIn is like having an online Rolodex.

4. Weekly status update email. You can update your "status" once a week, and from there LinkedIn will email everyone in your professional network in their weekly email updates about what you are doing that week. LinkedIn will also send you updates about articles that you will find relevant to your industry, as well as who in your network recently got hired in a new position. This can be used to help you gain introductions to certain companies and land you your next job! You can never have too many opportunities to stay at the forefront of a potential employer's mind.

5. Increased visibility. Having a LinkedIn profile increases your overall visibility, including raising your visibility on Google. This can help if a potential employer Googles your name before they bring you in for an interview.

**What to make sure is in your profile.** The first thing I do as a recruiter when I am looking to fill a position is to do a search on LinkedIn. I am consistently amazed by the quality and caliber of candidates who are now posting their profiles on LinkedIn. If you want your profile to be found on LinkedIn and you want to be the one called for opportunities, then there are a few key things you need to know about what recruiters and hiring managers are looking for:

• *Does the person have a complete profile, including work history and a photo?*

A profile that looks only partially filled out does not give enough information and leaves the impression that you are not putting very much effort into looking desirable and hirable. This is important because if you do not have a photo it could make the hiring manager wonder what you are trying to hide. I get people who often ask me, "What if the company will use that photo to discriminate against me?" This is a valid concern. What I explain to job seekers is that if a company is going to discriminate against you based on a photo, they are going to be just as likely to discriminate against you when they meet you in person. Personally, I would not want to work for that type of company to begin with. Also, please be sure to post a professional photo.

Many people do not put much thought into their photo on LinkedIn. Some people choose not to post a photo, period. I highly recommend having a photo on your LinkedIn profile as it can have people feel more related to you; however, if the photo is inappropriate, it can have the opposite effect.

The top five mistakes that I see when it comes to posting photos on your LinkedIn profile include the following:

1. Too sexy
2. Not professional (you do not have to be in a suit, but you should still stay away from overly casual clothes in your profile photo)
3. Distracting hair/makeup/jewelry—anything too over-the-top can take away from your presence
4. Blurred photos
5. Unfriendly face

Any one of the top five mistakes can lead an employer not to call your or pass on you altogether. When in doubt, phone a friend! Have several friends look at your profile photo and ask them if they would want to work with you based on that photo. If you keep your photo simple, clear and warm, you will be good to go!

- *Is this person's Summary completely filled out, including the type of position they are looking for?*

Often I come across a LinkedIn profile that does not have anything but the basics, that is, company, position and title. Not having your profile completely filled out makes it hard for a recruiter to ascertain whether you would be a fit for their position. Less is more does NOT apply to your LinkedIn profile.

- *Does the person have one or more strong recommendations from reliable LinkedIn sources?*

Having recommendations on LinkedIn is essential. If you cannot provide a supervisor reference, at the very least you should have a peer reference. One of the reasons that they are so highly valued is that it is very hard to falsify them. I would recommend having at least one recommendation per position you have held over the past five years.

- *Has this person been endorsed by their peers?*

LinkedIn recently added an "endorsement" section to the profile page. This gives your peers an opportunity to click a button to endorse you for a particular skill. It is step below a recommendation, but still has clout when it comes to how employers perceive your profile.

- *How hard is it going to be for me to connect with this person?*

Does this person clearly list their email address on their public LinkedIn profile? YES! You can do this by choosing to make your contact information public in your settings. I recommend listing a personal email address as opposed to a professional email.

- *Is this person connected to groups?*

If you are connected to groups it is much easier to connect with people then if you are not. Joining groups is an easy way to make you more visible to a potential employer. A member who does not know you can easily connect with you by stating that you are part of the same group. LinkedIn allows its non-paying members to connect to up to fifty groups. I recommend each person on LinkedIn connect to the maximum number. You can also join various groups on LinkedIn and start discussions within those groups, which also helps to raise your visibility. Starting discussions is also a great way to set yourself up as an expert in your field and can be a great way to make powerful new connections.

- *Does this person list at the bottom of their profile that they are interested in "career opportunities" or "job inquiries?"*

If a person does not list this on their profile, I might be more reticent to approach the person to begin with. They are probably not interested, and I do not want to waste my time.

- *Does this person list their current company?*

As a last resort, if the person has a complete profile, with recommendations, says they are interested in career opportunities, but do not list an email, at the very least I can try and reach them at their office if they have their current employer listed. Some recruiters may abuse this by aggressively trying to recruit someone from their current job. I use their business number to call and network with the person and find out how we can be a resource for one another.

If you are looking to change jobs and do not already have a LinkedIn profile, *please* put one together as soon as possible. Many people I know are landing interviews and job offers due to their LinkedIn profiles. I hire several people a year utilizing LinkedIn as one of my top resources. If you follow the above recommendations, you will be much more likely to be approached by a hiring company or recruiter regarding your dream job!

**LinkedIn recommendations.** I was once asked a very important question at a Pink Slip Mixer: "Should I have recommendations on my LinkedIn Profile and how important are they?" The answers are unequivocally *yes* and *very important!*

You are simply more likely to be hired if you have recommendations. Recommendations on LinkedIn are taken very seriously as it is nearly impossible to fake a LinkedIn recommendation. If a company Googles you and sees that you have several recommendations via LinkedIn, they will likely look on your application much more favorably. A company could also be concerned if you do not have any recommendations, so it is always advisable to have at least one recommendation—preferably one per job you have held!

In today's technologically advanced world, it is critical to make sure your online profile puts your best foot forward. If a potential employer comes across three potential candidates on LinkedIn and only one has good recommendations, who do you think is going to get the job?

This was the case for a senior paralegal I have worked with for years. Per my insistence, she not only put together a LinkedIn profile, but also went out and got several glowing recommendations as well. When she was called in for a high-level position with a law firm, and was asked to provide references, she was able to quickly direct them to her LinkedIn profile. The job offer, which came next, was due in part to the employer's ability to quickly verify those recommendations.

If you are on LinkedIn it is not acceptable not to have recommendations. Everyone should have at least one great recommendation if not three to five. This may seem like one of the more intimidating aspects of the profile, since it is a large one and one of the only ones that you the job seeker do not have direct control over.

Getting recommendations on LinkedIn is easier than it sounds, though—most people are even happier to do them when asked than they are for references. Recommending current or former colleagues of your own is a great way to inspire goodwill, generate connections, build a good reputation and encourage people to write recommendations for you.

**When to endorse.** I find it interesting how casually people are taking the endorsement function on LinkedIn. I am surprised by how many people are endorsing one another that have never even worked together or seen one another's work product. I find that people are arbitrarily endorsing others, without realizing that they are vouching for someone's skills. My thought process on whether or not to give an endorsement is that you should only endorse someone when they fall into one of the following five categories:

1. You have worked directly with that person at the same company and have seen their work firsthand.

2. You have hired them to do work for you and the results that they have produced have been above average.

3. They have hired you to do work for them as a vendor and you have seen the quality of their work.

4. You are a recruiter who has placed an individual in a job and know firsthand from your client that they have the skills that they purport to possess.

5. If you have worked against someone in a case or matter and have seen the quality of their work.

I think that endorsements should be taken seriously, just like you would take giving someone a reference or a recommendation seriously. So before you endorse someone the next time you are on LinkedIn, ask yourself if they fall into one of the five categories listed above.

**Avoid common LinkedIn errors.**   Although LinkedIn is a wonderful tool that, when used properly, can be instrumental in helping you land your next job, often people misunderstand how to effectively use it, and that can come back to hurt them in the long run. Here are a few things to consider when using LinkedIn:

- Having an incomplete profile can hurt you. LinkedIn has a lot of "Google Juice." This means that if your name is even remotely unique, and you have created a profile on LinkedIn, it will likely be the first or second thing that pops up when someone Google searches you. It is for this very reason that you want to make sure you have a complete profile that reflects who you are in the best possible light. You should create an online brand that represents who you are and what you offer in an effective, cohesive and consistent way.

- No profile photo = Less connections. People are less inclined to connect with people who do not have a profile picture. Not having a profile picture can discourage recruiters from wanting to contact you.

- Be careful whom you associate with. If someone has a bad reputation in your industry, or if a company or group is not looked upon positively, you might want to steer clear of connecting with that person or group via social media as it could reflect poorly upon you. Who you associate with says a lot about your personal brand and/or your business. You could be judged by whom you are connected with so make sure that you think twice before adding someone that could potentially tarnish your reputation.

- Not matching. Employers *will* search for you on LinkedIn, and if you have a profile that highlights your experience or qualifications in other fields, they are more likely to pass. Make sure your online presence matches what you're in the process of applying for, or potential employers will look askance at hiring someone from another field. Make sure you don't get yourself in trouble by listing things on your LinkedIn profile that are not on your resume or vice versa.

## Twitter—a little bird told me

You may already have a Twitter account. If so, perhaps you use it to message and keep in touch with your friends. But what you might be overlooking is that Twitter places one of the most potentially powerful marketing tools available right at your fingertips. Remember—making yourself attractive to employers basically consists of a marketing campaign for yourself, and Twitter can provide you with the exposure, platform and tools you need to make the campaign a success. Take a look through the following if you're not yet sold.

### The top three reasons to use Twitter

1. **Higher Google ranking.** Each "tweet" is treated by Google as an individual web page. This means that if you use your first and last name as your Twitter Username (*e.g.,* JenHillJHCCS), then you will automatically rank higher on Google the more often you tweet. This is important because employers are constantly

Googling potential employees to see what they can find out. This helps enormously—especially if you are tweeting about something related to your profession or industry.

2. **Company research.** Twitter is a very easy way to connect with people you might otherwise never get a chance to know. For example, you could begin to follow people within a certain organization you are interested in getting hired at. By following these employees, you can easily glean important information about the potential employer to help you get an interview and/or to find out if this is really the type of company you would like to work for. What is more, you can respond to the tweets of people who do not follow you, and often get a response back. This is a great way to start to connect with people from a business where you might want to apply.

3. **Follow trends.** Twitter is an excellent tool to keep up on trends in your industry and breaking news. Almost instantly, you can see what topics are trending and what breaking news is happening in your field. An example of how this could be useful in a job search would be to check Twitter prior to an interview, and see what topics are trending. Then when you are in the interview, you will have some interesting ice-breakers to share and will appear to have your finger on the pulse of what is happening in your profession.

## Facebook is not just for friends

Yes, I have left the most popular social network in the world for last. Chances are you already have a Facebook profile—but there is a good chance that you are not using it in a way that could help land you a good job!

When Facebook first came out, it was a great way to connect with old high school and college friends who you had lost touch with. Now that things have become more challenging with the economy, people are looking for new and innovative ways to find a job.

A concern that is often posed to me about using Facebook in your job search is: "I do not want my friends or family to know I am looking." The fact that you are looking for a job is nothing to be ashamed of.

It is just what is so. You would probably be surprised at how many of your college and high school friends would be happy to help you in whatever way they can. In the last year, since things have been tough, people have been banding together in support of one another in ways we would have never thought possible.

It is important to realize that your friends are your resources. Ask them, using your status update, if they might have any leads for you or perhaps be able to introduce you to someone at that special company you have been trying to get in the door with. Keep in mind that a majority of jobs are found through word of mouth, not through recruiters or job postings. Often a company will ask for internal referrals first, and the people they are asking are your friends on Facebook!

I would like to mention one caveat about using Facebook. If you are still employed, be careful about posting status updates regarding your job search. Even if you think your profile is private, your employer may know someone that has access to your profile and find out you are looking!

The next time you go onto Facebook to update your status, remember, it can be a useful tool in helping you to find your next job! Remember—the more people know you are looking for a job, the more people have a chance of giving you one!

For all the benefits of social networks, however, every asset has a potential disadvantage that must be avoided. Consider this story:

> Lily's excited about looking for a new job, and has just finished a polished resume that puts her past in the best possible light. She has had the opportunity to take some time off from working, and has put a lot of thought into where she will fit in the workforce. She has submitted her resume to employers that are all good fits and is looking forward to a response, but hears nothing. Hiring managers' attention had been caught by her strong resume presentation, so they first thing they did was to search for her Facebook page—where they found that her hobbies included S&M and that her profile photo was one of her provocatively dressed, holding a cocktail.

Many of us think of social networking sites as a way to communicate with our groups of friends while on the go or as a means of self-expression—but this can make it very easy to forget that an outlet such as a Facebook page can be a very public page on the Internet, as accessible to potential employers as the front page of CNN.com. Employers know that you will (and should be!) putting your best foot forward in everything you show them, and they will not want to miss an opportunity to see what you are like with your guard down. Perhaps not every solitary person who sees your resume will check to see if you have a Facebook page—but it is a good idea to assume they will. If what you show them reflects badly on you, it can sour your impression on hiring managers, as well as give the impression of apathy about how you come across.

Some things to avoid making public on social networking pages while looking for a job or representing a company include:

- **Drinking.** What may seem to you and your friends like a harmless glass of wine with dinner may taste more like vinegar to a lot of possible employers. Most companies have strict anti-alcohol policies; even while off the clock you do not want to give the appearance of flouting them. An employer will favor an applicant who gives an impression of responsibility—and alcohol is rarely associated with responsible behavior.

- **Illegal activities.** It may seem like a no-brainer, but many people think nothing of mentioning to friends how they have skirted the law—from downloading movies and music from illegal sources, to using recreational drugs, to trying to get out of paying taxes or a parking ticket. Businesses have rules that need to be followed, so they value people who know how to obey them. It may only have been jaywalking, but posting about it could show you in the opposite light.

- **Your politics.** Maybe you do not like that obnoxious major political candidate, or the president's foreign policy. Perhaps you feel very strongly on a hot button social issue. Even if all your friends agree with you (and they probably won't), the person who reads your resume very well may not. What is more, many companies have strong business reasons for remaining politically neutral, and they will want to see future employees who are capable of that. Unless you are applying to work for a political party, keep your politics to yourself.

- **Interpersonal feuds.** In a very real sense, social networking sites are really enormous gossip engines, and gossip occasionally has the tendency to become mean-spirited. If you get in a fight with a friend, do not air your dirty laundry on the Internet. If you were choosing an employee, would you want the candidate who stirred up trouble and bore grudges, or the one who seemed to get along well with everyone else? Employers will go for the second choice every time they have a chance.

This might seem stifling, but it could be the difference between getting the call and hearing nothing—and that should be worth one fewer friend request. Here are some tips to reduce the chances of letting something slip on social networks that you may not want a future boss to see:

- **Use a private name.** For example, most teachers use their first name and middle name, rather than using their first name and last name. They do this so that their students will not be able to find them. In this way, their harder-to-find page is one that only friends know about and a potential employer would have a harder time identifying.

- **Understand the privacy settings.** Facebook and many other social networking sites feature advanced privacy controls that can filter what you post only to your friends, only to certain groups of friends and by the type of post you are making. It is easy to overlook these controls, but it pays to get to know them when it matters who is reading what you post.

- **Communicate through other methods.** Initiating conversations with your friends via email or over the phone instead of posting on their Facebook wall makes it much less likely that you or someone else will accidentally leave something unsavory on public view.

- **Focus your main online presence on a more professional network.** Drawing attention to your presence on a network such as LinkedIn will help focus your content on more professional material, get you more online connections that will be useful in networking for business and help you develop an online profile that will be useful on its own.

Whether or not you know it, employers are Googling you. You need to be aware of who you are connected with on various social media sites and what others can or cannot see on your profile.

Whether you are employed or unemployed, it is important to be cognizant of what your social media profiles can say about you. If you are employed, you have to be careful about what you say about your workplace, colleagues or business related to the company or its clients. If you are complaining about your business or posting that you are looking for a job or out partying, an employer can have cause to fire you.

The same is true if you are unemployed and looking for a job. Employers take into consideration your photos, your wall posts and much more when evaluating whether they want to hire you or even interview you. The best course of action is to make your profile confidential on Facebook while you are looking for a job so that something you said or posted doesn't come back to haunt you.

## Other social media

As I am sure you have experienced, there is a mountain of social media data out there to try to make sense of. It has now become part of my job to help disseminate what information you need to know. The following are my top three additional social media tools that I feel are worth your time to investigate.

1. www.mashable.com. This is the "how to" guide/blog for using social media. In my opinion, I think it may be one of the most valuable sites out there for any social media questions you may have.

2. www.hootsuite.com. This site is a "Twitter Dashboard." It allows you to see who is tweeting both about you and to you. It helps you

organize your tweets by scheduling them in advance, and keeping track of who is retweeting your messages. You can also use this to help shrink your URLs so that you can get more bang for your buck. The less work you have to put into basic tasks on Twitter, the more you can get out of it.

3. www.ning.com. This site allows you to build your own social network. It can be a business endeavor or it can be just for fun. Either way, it is a great way to further showcase your interests and talents. Knowing how to start something from the ground up is often the best step to understanding it—and it is impossible to emphasize enough how important an understanding of social networking is in this day and age.

## Social media dos and don'ts

Finally, before we move on from social media, let's take a look at some simple but easy-to-overlook dos and don'ts that will be important for you to remember as you take advantage of this technology.

- Don't post something on someone else's profile or your own that could get you or them in trouble (even if your profile is set to confidential information can still get out!).

- Do post messages on people's profiles related to special occasions— this is a great way to show you care.

- Don't over post on your own wall or site—people hate information overload!

- Do carefully choose what you post and how often you post it. (Always use the 30/30/30 rule: 30% personal, 30% professional & 30% sharing helpful information—the last 10% should be spent commenting on and liking other people's posts.)

- Do keep a consistent "voice" that authentically expresses who you are across all social media sites.

- Don't try to be someone you are not—people see right through inauthenticity!

## 30% APPLYING TO JOBS ONLINE

It may seem obvious once it is stated, but it is a step skipped over by a surprising number of job seekers: Before you start applying, you have to have a good idea of what kind of place you would like to work at. Before spending valuable time sending out resumes to shot-in-the-dark companies at which you may not want to work, know the kind of work you want to do, and the kind of place you want to do it in. If you do not know for sure, start thinking about the things you know you can do well, or the kinds of work and volunteer experience you already have.

It may be helpful to take a personality test to help determine what sort of work you are best suited for or might most enjoy. Probably the most popular personality test over time has been the one called Myers-Briggs, which is available on the Internet.

However you do it, you will want to have a strong idea going into your job search of just what sort of work you're looking for. This makes it miraculously easier to find the right places to apply, and it leads me back to one of your first pieces of **homework**: *Make a Wishlist about your ideal job so you will know when you have found it.* See the earlier section entitled "Where Do I Even Begin" on what your ideal Wishlist should look like and how you can incorporate it into your job search.

This will not just help you with finding the right places to apply and—once you have got the job—with knowing which kind of position to accept and which kind of job to stay at, but it will also give you plenty of ripe fodder when your eventual interviewer asks those inevitable and all-important questions: Why do you want to work here? Do you have any questions for us?

### Listings—Monster, CareerBuilder or Indeed?

Websites such as www.monster.com and www.careerbuilder.com tend to be very well known from advertising and from other associated publicity, but they have a system that generally presents you with one job listing at a time. Your goal at this stage should be to find as many listings as possible so you can sort the wheat from the chaff yourself to find the best places for you as an employee.

To that end www.monster.com and www.careerbuilder.com should not be completely discounted, but you should also use aggregator search engines that allow you to enter your own criteria and generate a selection of listings drawn from multiple sources, essentially doing most of the work for you.

With new job-hunting websites popping up every day, it becomes harder and harder to discern which ones to use. One of my favorite tips for job seekers is to set yourself up with www.indeed.com job alerts. Indeed is powered by Google and thus is able to search *every* site on the web for the position you are looking for.

If you are not already on Indeed, I highly recommend setting yourself up with several job alerts. These alerts will be emailed to you every morning and will list every position that meets your search criteria. You want to make sure to set up several different alerts to match your profession as different recruiters and hiring managers will use different titles. For example, if you are an attorney, you might want to do one alert for "attorney," one for "lawyer," one for "associate" and so on.

There is a feature that allows you to post your resume on indeed. com; however, be cautious because as of right now, anyone can find your resume on the site. You do not want your potential employer to see you on there if you are still working. If you are unemployed, it could be beneficial to post your resume there.

A new website that I recently found is called "Linkup." I only became aware of this website in the last few months and have not had an opportunity to properly vet it, but it seems to have a unique corner in the marketplace. What I do know about Linkup is that the site allows you to passively search for unadvertised jobs. Linkup allows you to search a company's website directly for any positions that posted on its website, whereas most other job boards post only paid job advertisements. In my opinion, Linkup has the potential to be a great resource for finding out about the positions that no one else knows about.

## SHOULD YOU USE A RECRUITER?

Considering the effort that is needed to find the right job for you, it may occur to you to go to a recruiter. This is ultimately going to be your decision, and like anything, it is one that has its pros and cons. I have compiled a list of these to help you evaluate your options.

*Why should you use a recruiter?*
- Using a recruiter can be beneficial when you are working in a specialized area. Recruiters often help companies find candidates for hard-to-fill, specialized positions.

- When you are looking for temporary work. If you are looking to supplement your income a recruiter can be a great resource. When you register with an agency it will keep you on its active list and keep you updated on any contract jobs that meet your job search criteria.

- A recruiter can often provide you with resources such as testing and internal information on specific companies and hiring managers that can help you land your next job.

- A recruiter can critique your resume and can offer valuable information regarding what companies are looking for. Additionally, a recruiter can offer excellent interviewing tips prior to your interviews.

- A recruiter will typically negotiate your salary for you.

- A recruiter may have access to job openings that you will not find on Monster, CareerBuilder or other typical resources. A recruiter can tell you about personalities and key attributes the firm or company is looking for.

- One of the main reasons a job seeker might want to consider using a recruiter is that using a recruiter is free to the job seeker. Companies pay recruiters to find them the right candidates, but recruiters typically do not charge a job seeker to represent them.

- More and more companies are utilizing recruiters to hire people, and if you are NOT working with a recruiter, they might not consider your resume.

- A recruiter's job is to sell you and your background to the company. It is much harder to get yourself into a company just based on your resume. A recruiter can use preexisting relationships to help sell you and your background.

- A recruiter can also offer valuable training and tutorials to help you progress in your career.

## Why should you be careful of using a recruiter?

- A bad recruiter can send your resume out to potential employers WITHOUT your permission and/or knowledge. Keep in mind that, unlike financial professionals, recruiters do not report to any regulatory agency. It is your job to interview recruiters and to make sure they are looking out for your best interests before you decide to move forward working with them.

- Be careful about posting your resume on Monster and Career-Builder! Recruiters can find your resume on those sites and send your resume out without your knowledge.

- Set rules and realistic expectations with your recruiter up front. Let your recruiter know in advance that you want to have every position run by you first before your resume is sent out. Ideally, you should have an Excel spreadsheet with *where* your resume has been sent, to *whom* it has been sent, *when* it was sent, to *what* company it was sent, and if a recruiter did send your resume, be sure to list *which* agency represented you for that position.

- Recruiters have anywhere from a six-month to a one-year contract with each company they work with. This is why it is important to always know which agency sent you for a particular position. If ABC agency sent your resume to XYZ Company in May, and now XYZ Company has another position posted in July, you will be obligated to go through ABC agency again if you want to pursue that opportunity. This is not always a bad thing, but it is something you should be aware of and keep track of.

- If you are looking to make a career transition, a recruiter might not be the best resource for you. Recruiters are paid a fee by a company to find *exactly* what that company is looking for. This means recruiters might not have as much wiggle room to get a candidate an interview when that candidate's experience is not a direct fit.

Overall, recruiters can be a wonderful resource for you in your job search when used properly. Do not rely 100% on a recruiter to find you a job. They will do the best they can, but cannot find every job seeker a job every time. It is important to always be honest, patient and respectful with recruiters. If you are, you will reap the rewards!

## Choosing a recruiter

So, assuming you have decided that you do want to use a recruiter, you will of course want to choose the best one possible. It is important that you do your due diligence before committing. Finding the right recruiter to fit your personality should not be work, but if you do not choose wisely, your decision could have long-term implications on your career. As in other areas, there are good recruiters and bad recruiters. The question is: How do you tell the difference?

In order to find a recruiter who is looking out for your best interests and not just for their next paycheck, there are a few things to consider. The first thing you want to look at is: Does this recruiter specialize in my field? There are as many recruiters out there as there are jobs so it is important to find one who works in your particular field. If you are in the IT world, you would want someone who is tech savvy and knows the type of technology you are dealing with. Ask your recruiter what areas they specialize in and see if they line up with your skill set.

The next thing to think about is: Should I trust this person? Many recruiters become so excited by a good resume that they will not dot their I's and cross their T's. You need to take the time to meet with your recruiter whenever possible, and be sure that your recruiter takes the time to get to know you and what you are looking for in your next position. If a recruiter simply wants to send your resume out without taking the time to understand what you want, chances are they are just looking to make a quick buck. Be sure to emphasize that you do not want your resume sent *anywhere* without your permission. If your resume is sent to an employer without your knowledge this can hurt you in the long run if you apply to that company later on your own or through a recruiter you do like.

Once you have established that your recruiter is trustworthy and specializes in your field, see if that recruiter can provide recommendations. Now, I want to be clear, most recruiters will not appreciate it if you call them asking for a list of references. If instead you ask them where you can find recommendations on them I am sure they will be happy to direct you to their LinkedIn profile or website where they should have at least one or multiple recommendations.

## Working with your recruiter

You want to make absolutely sure to have a good relationship with your recruiter rather than an antagonistic one. Remember—this is the person whose goal is to be the gateway to you getting a job! What are the things you need to know about how to effectively work with a recruiter?

1. Do not be afraid to use your recruiter as a resource to find out information about the market. Recruiters have their fingers on the pulse of what is happening with their niche market.

2. Always be 100% honest with your recruiter about everything from your academic credentials to your past employment. If a recruiter finds out that you lied to them, they will likely not work with you again or, worse, blacklist you. Even if your lie gets past a recruiter for now, it can only come back to haunt you later.

3. Work with your recruiter to help them understand your ideal job, and in that way they will not waste your time by sending you out on interviews for positions that are not the right fit. Work with your recruiter on making sure they understand what is on your "Wishlist."

4. Expect that your recruiter will likely call you anywhere from a couple of times a week to once a month depending on how hot your industry is.

5. Most recruiters should prepare you for interviews by giving you inside information about what to expect and interview tips, but not all do.

6. As discussed earlier, you will be expected to meet with a recruiter in person. In some cases they may administer a test to you if you are more junior or if the client requires it. If you are looking to get a position out of the area then you should get Skype so that you can interview with out-of-state recruiters.

7. Never waste your time or your recruiter's time by going on interviews that are not of interest to you. If a recruiter presents an opportunity to you that does not interest you, then do not have them submit your resume in the first place. Also, if you are confirmed for an interview, you must give at least 24 hours' notice to cancel the interview (unless an emergency comes up). However, cancelling interviews in general can make you appear flaky and unreliable. If you cancel or reschedule more than one interview, a recruiter may not want to represent you again.

8. Recruiters will negotiate your salary and will present you with opportunities as they arise. Be clear with your recruiter about your current compensation and what you expect to be compensated in your next position. Your current compensation can be verified and if it is misrepresented by you or the recruiter, you might have your job offer rescinded.

9. Do not expect your recruiter to always be the first to call you. There may be 100 or more recruiters in Los Angeles, but there are thousands of job seekers. The phone rings both ways; do not be afraid to check in every now and again. Always check your recruiter's website for new postings and email the recruiter if you see something that might be a fit or that would potentially interest you.

10. Do not take it personally if your recruiter does not call you for a position that they called someone else for. They may have not gotten around to calling you yet or they might not have thought it was the best fit for you based on your "Wishlist."

*Recruiters do not work for you. They work for the companies who pay them!* It is important to remember that recruiters work for free for the job

seekers and that they do their best to accommodate everyone that they can. Please be considerate and respectful of a recruiter's time. A recruiter who is treated well can be your best ally. Even though a recruiter does not work for you, he or she does have the same goal—getting you the most appropriate job!

## Help your recruiter to help you

In order for recruiters to be effective at placing you, they need your help. There are a few things you can do to help a recruiter get you a job:

- Clearly communicate any and all feedback, both good and bad, following any interview so that they can help negotiate and get you the job if you want it or gracefully decline if you are not interested.
- Let your recruiter know well in advance if there is a potential issue with your background check such as bad credit or a DUI. It is better for a recruiter to let the client company know about an issue up front if an offer is to be made; typically if the company is alerted early enough, the issue is not a big deal as long as you are honest about it.
- Never lie to your recruiter.
- Let your recruiter know about any preexisting vacations so that they can alert an employer if necessary.
- Be sure you can provide a minimum of at least one reference and ideally three to five references that can be called. Reference "letters" are useless in today's society and age. If you cannot provide a reference for the hiring manager to speak with, then you might not be able to be hired.
- Always be on time and research the company you are interviewing with in advance.

There are additional things you can do to help a recruiter help you if you are unemployed. These can help a recruiter place you in a temporary-to-hire position or temporary situation:

- Let your recruiter know if and when you are available for temporary or temporary-to-hire assignments. Often the people who

check in once a week are the ones who get called first for a job. Email is always preferable.

- Be extremely flexible and accommodating on the first day of any temporary or temporary-to-hire assignment. This includes offering to help others, asking questions, and not complaining about anything unless you are doing so directly with your recruiter and not the employer. Keep in mind, you are not hired until an offer is made.

- Do not ever bring up benefits or salary on a temporary assignment. If an employer brings these things up with you, that is acceptable, but it is inappropriate for you to broach the subject directly with the employer.

- Do not push the employer to hire you directly. This typically turns the employer off. Always communicate directly with your recruiter regarding the status of your employment.

- If you are ever going to be late or out, always notify your recruiter.

## PUT THE WORK INTO APPLYING

It may seem pretty straightforward, but it is often overlooked: The quickest way not to land a job is not to apply for it. Job seeking is an area where putting the effort in really makes an appreciable difference, and no matter how low you think your chances are of being hired for a particular position, they do not go down to zero unless you don't bother applying.

When you are looking for a job, you should consider looking for a job to be your full-time job. Apply to a minimum of five to ten jobs per day and keep yourself to a full-time schedule: Spend at least 40 hours each week on your job search, if you are unemployed. There is strength in numbers, and, quite simply, the more positions you apply for the more offers you will get and the more choices you will have.

Put the same effort into every application as you would for your dream job. If it is not worth the work of applying, it is not a job worth having. Fill out every application thoroughly. Do not write "see attached resume"—if you treat the interview like a cookie-cutter process, the interviewer will treat you the same way.

## TAKE IT ONE DAY AT A TIME

*"The best thing about the future is that it comes one day at a time."*
                                        *Abraham Lincoln*

It is easy to get distracted from your job search by everyday things. Your family, your friends and a variety of other commitments are just waiting to pull you away from your job search. When you are looking for a job it is important to stay focused and to not lose sight of what you are committed to—finding a job. The longer you have been looking for a job, the more challenges and distractions you may find that you are faced with. Here are a few tips for staying motivated and focused in your job search:

- The most important thing that you can do to stay focused in your job search is to set yourself up with a schedule, just like you would if you were in the office, and stick to it! Granted, there will be times where you will need to adjust the schedule, but overall, having a set schedule will help you have some sense of normalcy.

- Wake up every morning and give yourself at least five minutes to focus on what you want to accomplish that day before you do anything else. If you spend each morning thinking about what you want to accomplish it will help you to focus your day on what needs to get done and will help you to plan more effectively. I also suggest starting every day by doing your "Daily Declaration," which will be covered in more depth in Part 5: The Mental Side of Your Search.

- Check your email first thing in the morning. It is important not to miss out on any important job interviews that may have come up. It is also important to check your email first thing in the morning because many websites such as www.indeed.com and www.jobshouts.com offer features that will send you an updated email with any new positions that have come up in the last 24 hours (this email is typically sent out first thing in the morning). It is important to jump on these opportunities when they are fresh so that you are at the top of the pile of those who are being considered.

- Apply to jobs in the morning. Do not put off sending in your resume until the end of the day. Remember, the early bird gets the worm and you do not want to miss out on your dream job because you put off applying to a particular position until it was too late! Recruiters and hiring managers are often inundated with resumes, and may find what they are looking for in the first hundred resumes that are submitted. Resumes that are sent later in the day can often be lost in the shuffle.

- Only spend an hour or two a day using social media and use that time intentionally. Once you have found the jobs you are interested in and have sent your resume out to those jobs, it is now time to use LinkedIn, Facebook and Twitter to help facilitate your job search. Use this time wisely! Tweet about relevant articles in your industry, use LinkedIn to start discussions related to your field and, finally, connect with Facebook friends to see who they might know that could be a resource for you. Try to avoid going onto these websites more than once a day. Social media can be a wonderful tool to use in your job search, but it also can be a distraction if not used properly.

- Save the networking for evenings or later in the day. Networking can be a lot of fun and a great resource for finding a new job, but it can also take a lot of work and require a lot of energy. It is better to get your other work done first before you invest all of your energy by attending a networking event.

If you follow these steps and create a schedule that works for you, you will quickly find yourself with more free time and more of the results you want: Interviews!

## FIX YOUR MISTAKES—SILLY REASONS FOR GETTING PASSED UP

The other day my husband and I were driving to dinner. I was feeling a bit frustrated because one of the job seekers I was working with did not get the job she was applying for and the reason was something silly. This happens more often than I would like and my husband suggested, "Honey, why don't you start a list of some of the silliest and simplest reasons people have not gotten hired and share it with your candidates before they go to their interviews?"

At first I thought that some of these reasons might be too simple to mention, but it is the little things that make the biggest difference.

We are all human, and we all make "stupid" mistakes from time to time. The important thing is to remember that simple mistakes—while they can be the most embarrassing—are also the simplest to fix. If your job search involves being passed up for some jobs because of simple, absentminded mistakes, do not get discouraged—prevent or fix them and get the job on your next interview!

Here are some of the most frustrating—but easily fixable—mistakes that I have seen in my time as a recruiter:

- A job seeker went in for an interview and was wearing too short of a skirt. Needless to say, the client passed.
- A legal secretary misspelled the word "litigation" on a legal test.
- In the final stages of an interview, a candidate got the company name wrong.
- A job seeker went in for an interview and looked everywhere except at the interviewer (good eye contact is always critical!).
- A job seeker addressed the human resources person by the wrong name on more than one occasion.
- After looking for a job for over two years, a job seeker finally got an interview and showed up fifteen minutes late.
- A candidate passed every other test, but on one test, she second-guessed herself and changed a few of her answers at the last minute, which led to her failing one of the necessary tests and being passed on.
- During a phone screen a job seeker was asked to describe her typical day and was unable to clearly communicate what she did on a day-to-day basis.
- During another job seeker's phone interview, she did not know the answer to the question and proceeded to Google the answer in the middle of the interview, which the interviewer heard.
- During a third and final interview a candidate decided to wear perfume; the perfume was so overpowering that no one in the office thought they could work with her.

- A candidate went through five interviews with everyone in the company and after the final interview received an offer; however, she sent a thank you letter that looked something like this:

Hi ___!

I am really super excited to work for you ☺! This is exactly what I have always wanted to do ☺! Cannot wait to work with you!!!!

Job Seeker ☺

Needless to say, the company rescinded the offer—almost as fast as the company that got a thank you letter addressed to the wrong person! Thank you letters are a big help, but only if they are proofread and professional!

## ONE BLANK LINE COULD COST YOU THAT JOB

I recently learned a very important lesson in recruiting and career coaching. Never think that any advice is too obvious. I have been recruiting and coaching now for close to ten years and the longer I have been in the business the more I notice I take it for granted that job seekers know certain things. One such thing came to my attention today.

I had thoroughly prepared a job seeker for her interview with a law firm. She knew how to answer just about any question you threw at her; however, the one thing I did not prepare her for was how to fill out the application. I was reminded that I need to cover *everything* from the application to the thank you note when I prepare candidates for an interview. You might think the application itself it as simple as filling out your answers on a questionnaire, but there are opportunities and pitfalls everywhere!

This candidate was so well prepared on how to answer her reason for leaving her past position that when it came time to answer that question on the application, she thought there was not enough space to fully answer the question the way I had coached her and she left it blank. This is my fault. I should have let her know what I am about to tell you: NEVER LEAVE A QUESTION BLANK ON AN APPLICATION! It is perfectly acceptable to put a short answer down on the application and then elaborate further when asked the question directly.

One of the biggest pet peeves of many human resources professionals is not thoroughly completing your job application. You should *always* thoroughly answer any question on the application. *Never* put "see attached resume" or leave a question blank. This makes you look lazy or disinterested, which is the last thing you want to convey in an application. In a worst-case scenario you could always put "open" or "negotiable" if the question has to do with salary desired or hours preferred.

In these economic times, it is also important to be prepared for a background check. Some companies will require you to fill out their background check form during the first interview. This does *not* mean they are going to run your background check right then; most companies will keep it on file and run it *only* if they offer you the job. If not, they will simply shred it.

Do not give the hiring manager a reason not to hire you. Be thorough and complete and please be accommodating with any requests they make of you when it comes to filling out background check information.

## TIPS FOR KEEPING UP YOUR JOB SEARCH MORALE

I network with hundreds of job seekers each month. I find that a lot of them have trouble avoiding the temptation to become disconsolate and distraught from months and months of job hunting without seeing the results they want. Following are some suggestions of things you can do to boost your confidence and morale, and possibly make a little extra money while doing them.

1. **Volunteer.** Volunteering is a great way to gain valuable experience to make yourself more marketable while at the same time contributing to your community. If you do not know what type of place you would like to volunteer at, or where to find volunteer opportunities, please check out www.volunteermatch.org.

2. **Join Toastmasters.** Joining Toastmasters is a great way to increase your confidence and your ability to communicate clearly. This is an extremely important tool to master for interviews and in networking situations. To find your local Toastmasters go to www. toastmasters.org.

3. **Join Meetup and/or networking groups.** People often become depressed from sitting at home and not having the social element that they are used to from having a job. A great way to combat this feeling of loneliness is to join a networking group such as www.meetup.com or a job-hunting networking group like www.pinkslipmixers.com.

4. **Take classes.** Have you ever wanted to learn photography, writing or graphic design? There is no time like the present. You can take classes at UCLA, Santa Monica College, Westwood College, University of Phoenix or find a local college in your area that offers classes on a subject that interests you by going to www.college. com. You may even discover an interest that leads to a new career, or gain experience and qualifications that could help you in your professional life.

5. **Start up an MLM business.** Some people may scoff at multi-level-marketing businesses, but the reason there are so many out there is because they work! With such a wide variety of products and business types, you have a plethora of choices of what type of business to go into and how much you want to invest. Some MLMs may require a significant investment, but others you can start for as little as $30 a year. To find the right one for you go to www.mlmrankings.com.

6. **Mystery shop.** Not a lot of people are familiar with mystery shopping, or at least they do not talk about it for obvious reasons. Mystery shopping can be a fast, easy and fun way to earn some extra money. In some cases you can even get reimbursed for food and lodging. Mystery shopping is not for everyone, as you have to be very observant and detail oriented, but for some, it is a great way to help supplement your income. Be careful of scams! Some good websites to check out are www.mysteryshop.org, www.sassieshop. com and www.bestmark.com.

7. **Take on freelance/contract work.** Contract work is a great way to gain experience and knowledge in a field you might not be as strong in, check out a company's atmosphere, as well as offer you a chance to have a flexible schedule and make money at the same time. A few great ways to find contract work are through utilizing

recruiters or checking out websites like www.jobsdirectusa.com or www.elance.com. It's also a great way to build contacts in a company and gain the trust of people who already work there.

8. **Start a blog.** Blogging is not for everyone, although I highly recommend it if you want to share experiences and work towards being an expert in your field. There is no easier, cheaper way to become an expert than by blogging. It is important to choose a subject that inspires you and that you will want to write about every month. I personally recommend blogging at least once a week. One great website to use for blogging is www.wordpress.com.

9. **Join a focus group.** Focus groups are a great way to get paid while you job hunt. Some focus groups will pay anywhere from $100–300 for participating in a particular focus group. It is a great way to get out and meet people, as well as make money while you job hunt. One example of a focus group company you can join is www.focuspointeglobal.com.

10. **Start a business.** Starting your own business may seem daunting at first, but it can be a wonderful way to help you make money while you are looking for a full-time job. You never know, you might even wind up doing your new business full time. Chances are you already are an expert in one area or another. You can take that expertise and launch a consulting business. Social media tools like www.twellow. com, www.facebook.com and www.twitter.com make it simple to advertise for free and get your name out there. To learn more about how to start your own small business go to http://www.sba.gov/category/navigation-structure/starting-managing-business.

# 3 | Innovative Ways to Get Hired

*"Innovation distinguishes between a leader and a follower."*

Steve Jobs

## VOLUNTEER

If you are in search of a steady paycheck, volunteering might not be the first thing that comes to mind. But it is an important action to consider, especially for those looking to get back to work after a period of unemployment. What employers care about is not so much seeing an uninterrupted history, but seeing that you have been continually making good, productive use of your time. Showing that you have been volunteering is leagues better than leaving a blank space anywhere in your work history.

In fact, you can use volunteering to turn what could be a detrimental gap in your resume into an asset—volunteer in a capacity that will gain you experience in an area you know you would like to pursue. If you know you want to be a sports reporter, contributing to a sports blog is a great way to get experience, practice and maybe even a reputation before you have secured a position. Here is one such story:

> Joan had been employed at a world-renowned law firm as a real estate legal secretary for over twenty-five years. When the real estate market crashed in 2009, she was laid off along with hundreds of others at her firm. She knew that it would take a while for the market to recover, so she decided to volunteer as an executive corporate secretary to a local charity. When the market finally started to rebound two years later and she still had not landed a full-time job or even a contract position, she was able to cite her volunteer work experience as what she had been doing to keep her skills fresh. The employer she interviewed with liked that she had kept herself busy volunteering and brought her on.

Volunteering shows employers that you are dedicated to being productive and that you are a self-starter—both very desirable qualities—and can in many cases help generate a body of work for them to evaluate. Remember that actions speak louder than words, so showing that you have what your prospective employer is looking for makes a far greater impact than just saying you have it.

Importantly, volunteering in the area where you will be looking for work is a great way for you network and make connections in that industry. It is impossible to overstate the importance of "who you know," and if you are looking to make inroads into an industry where you do not already have a great deal of experience, there is no better way than to get involved in some volunteer projects.

Of course, this advice does not just apply if you are unemployed and would otherwise end up with a gap in your work history. If you are looking to switch career tracks and join a new industry, volunteering in the area that interests you most can be just as vital.

When you volunteer, should you add your volunteer experience to your resume? Always!

There are two possible situations:

- In the first situation, you may still be employed and looking for another job. If the volunteer work you are doing while working is NOT in the field that you are looking to get into, then you do not need to list the volunteer work as a position on your resume. In that situation, your volunteer work can go at the bottom of your resume under accomplishments, hobbies, interests, groups, associations, etc. If you are doing volunteer work in a field that you currently have no experience in, and are looking to transition into, then it is a good idea to list your volunteer work as an actual position under your "Work Experience."

- In the second situation, you are unemployed and looking for a job. The longer you have been out of work, the more important it is to show something on your resume to explain what you have been doing since your last job. This could be temporary or contract work, or if you volunteer, you can list your volunteer experience as your most recent position. Employers like to see that you have been doing something since you got laid off.

It is important to note that when you list your volunteer work on your resume you should put (Volunteer) next to your experience so that there is no confusion!

Remember, volunteer work can be just as important as paid work, especially when you are learning new and valuable skills.

## SO YOU HAVE NEVER VOLUNTEERED . . .

If I have convinced you to spend some time volunteering while you are looking for your dream job, you might not have any experience that leads you to know how to go about it. There are two different ways to go about volunteering. One way is to find any charitable organization or cause that you believe in and to offer any skills you can to support the company or organization. Another way to volunteer is to specifically target companies that you want to work for and offer your services free of charge so that you can keep your skills fresh or gain new skills in an area in which you are interested. Remember, volunteering is an opportunity to do something that you really want to do—which could lead to a job doing what you really want to do while getting paid!

Once you have decided which direction you want to take your volunteering in, the next step is finding the company that needs your services. You can go to www.volunteermatch.org to find a list of charitable organizations that are always looking for volunteers.

If you are in sales, you might want to try your hand at fundraising. If you are an administrative professional you might want to offer administrative support. If you are looking to target specific companies you may want to utilize LinkedIn to find out who the appropriate party would be to reach out to and offer your pro bono services to. For example, if you were a legal assistant, you might want to look up solo practitioners on LinkedIn and reach out to attorneys who could potentially use your help and offer them assistance with filing or the like. You never know, it could turn into a full-time, paid position down the road.

The point is that good help is always hard to find! If you are a job seeker who wants to give back and add value to your resume, then I would suggest looking into different options of how you can volunteer.

## THE BUDDY SYSTEM

One more thing before I leave my discussion of finding the job itself. What if you have been looking for a job for more than six months? More than a year? If you have been looking for a job for an extended period of time, and have not seen the results you are looking for, then I have a suggestion I would like you to try. I call it "The Buddy System."

This is a straightforward job-hunting method with a new spin on it. Studies have shown that 80% of job seekers find jobs through casual acquaintances. Many people have heard of this statistic before, but how many job seekers have maximized its potential?

People often look for jobs within their circle of friends or connections. The only problem with this is that those people likely know the same people that you know, and so they may not be the best resource for you in your job search. I suggest broadening your network by finding yourself a "buddy" who is not part of your normal networking group, and who is also looking for a job. Networking events are great (more on that soon!), but eventually your circle of connections winds up overlapping because you attend many of the same events with the same people.

The buddy system is based on the principle that your goal is to get your buddy a job via introductions to appropriate parties, assist them with landing interviews, and by any other methods you can think of. In turn, your buddy should do the same for you. If each person commits to doing this for their buddy, the results will be astounding. It is like having your own personal PR agent promoting you and connecting you with people 24/7.

In order for you and your buddy to be the best possible resource for one another, I have a few suggestions to make:

- Find a buddy outside of your normal circle of connections by using social media sites such as LinkedIn and/or Twitter. Look for people with common interests and goals who live in your area. Try not to connect with people you already have a direct connection with, as your circles will likely already overlap.

- Once you have found this buddy and proposed your new symbiotic relationship to him or her, offer to meet with him or her so that you can get to know one another better. When you take the time to get to know your buddy better, it will help you each to become a better resource for the other.

- Do not choose a buddy completely out of your field, as he or she might not be able to represent you as effectively as possible if he or she does not understand your business and where you are coming from. For example, if you are in engineering, you might not want to choose someone in human resources as your buddy (unless they worked in HR at an engineering-related company) as they may not fully understand the scope of the work that you do.

- Check in with your buddy daily. You want to stay fresh in each other's minds, and communicate daily on the progress you are making. This will help you both to stay focused on your respective job searches and will give you a sense of accountability towards one another. You can also treat each other as confidants regarding what is happening with your job search. This can give you the sense of being part of a team, which can help to build confidence and alleviate stress.

- Finally, think of the buddy system as a game. Expectations are premade resentments. If you *expect* your buddy to find you a job, and stop doing the work yourself, you will be sorely disappointed. However, if you see the buddy system as a fun and effective way to broaden your circle of connections, and if you use it as such, it can be a powerful tool in helping you to land your next job.

## USE LEVERAGE

Leverage is an important concept that you will want to keep in mind during your job search. Think of a physical lever—you are using a tool to turn your own power into an action. That is the model you will be applying over and over again in your job search. As you look at the following three ways to use leverage in your job search, try to think of ways that the concept applies to other work that you do.

1. Leverage your time. This means that when you are online applying to various positions, take one or two minutes to update your status on your social media sites. One quick and easy way to update your status on all your social media sites at once is by using www.hootsuite.com. Hootsuite allows you to update your status on LinkedIn, Facebook, Twitter and many other sites all at the same time. By doing this you will be leveraging the time that you already are spending online.

2. Leverage your contacts. Use the contacts that you have! Many job seekers that I come across are afraid to let their network know that they are looking for a job, or they are shy about using their friends and family as networking tools. Many job seekers may be ashamed that they were laid off, or perhaps they do not think anyone in their network has the contacts they need. If you do not ask, you will not receive!

3. Leverage your knowledge. Whether you are a recent college graduate, or a seasoned professional in your field, we all have specialized knowledge. If you are a recent college graduate, you might have specific study methods that helped you ace your exams; if you just got laid off after more than twenty years as a project manager, you may have more knowledge then you know what to do with. In either case, start a blog! Blogging is one of the quickest and simplest ways to share the specialized knowledge you have with others. By doing so you might just capture the attention of a potential employer.

By using these three easy leveraging techniques, you will help to make yourself more visible to the people that want to hire you. In everything you do in your job search, you should be leveraging for current and future advantages.

## GET PAST THE GATEKEEPER!

One new method you might try for finding a job is to pick up the phone and call the hiring managers and/or executives directly. However, very few people are successful at using this technique, for a variety of reasons.

Having been a recruiter for over ten years, getting past gatekeepers was always one of my specialties. Being a recruiter requires you to be able to get past gatekeepers to the hiring managers in much the same way that a job seeker would try to bypass a gatekeeper. After many years of exploring what works and what does not, I have found a few specific things that you can do the next time you call a company that will assist you in getting past the gatekeeper. Here are some of my suggestions:

1. Have a LinkedIn profile. As we discussed, having a LinkedIn profile is a great way to gather the names of the people you want to contact, and also to find out information about the person that can help you to break the ice. In addition, you can use LinkedIn groups to connect with people you might otherwise have no connections with.

2. When you call a particular company, it is important not to use the full name of the person you are calling or attempt to address that person by Mr. or Mrs. For example, if you are trying to reach Bob Jones, the CEO of ABC Corporation, and you say to the receptionist "Is Mr. Jones available?" this is an immediate red flag. There are two reasons that calling the person by Mr./Mrs. or their full name can be a red flag:

   • If you call them Mr. or Mrs., this likely means you are not someone who ranks high on the list of people whose calls should be put through. Close acquaintances or business associates usually call each other by their first names. Also, if Bob had a more unique last name such as Remeinzski, and you mispronounced it, it would be rather obvious that you do not know Bob.

3. Do not launch into a story about who you are and why you are calling. Business associates, family members, and friends are short and to the point and expect to be put through, rather than rattling on about why they are calling. You want to create a sense that you already know Bob. An example of how to do this would be to say something to the effect of "Is Bob around?" Nothing complicated, just short and to the point. If they ask what it is regarding you could say, "I am just calling him back" or "I was just following up regarding an email." Less is more. There is no need to make a long-drawn-out complicated story.

Of course trying to get past the gatekeeper does have certain risks, and you need to be able to pull it off convincingly. For instance, I had a guy in sneakers and jeans show up wanting to meet with someone in my agency. I let him know his attire was unprofessional and that I highly recommended he at least put on dress slacks if he intended to try to work with agencies. On the flip side, I had another job seeker show up unannounced in a full suit wanting to speak with someone in my office, and he was given an immediate interview. Remember—the more you look and sound the part, the more likely you are to get the opportunity to play it in real life.

Generally these few tips will help you to get past the gatekeeper if executed properly. The key is confidence. If you sound like someone who should be speaking to the CEO, the chances are you will get the opportunity to. "Gatecrashing" the party can be a great way to get yourself in with the people at the top and bypass competition with the other applicants. It takes guts, but it can pay off.

## CONNECTING WITH EXECUTIVES

OK, so maybe you have crashed the gate and you are on the line with a very high-up person at the company where you want to work. Congratulations! Now ... what do you say? How do you make a connection?

I recently had an opportunity to listen to a speaker who also happens to be one of the world's greatest connectors. He is known throughout the world for his ability instantaneously to connect with multimillionaires and billionaires anywhere he goes. Part of what he attributes his success to is his attitude and another part of his success is his willingness to be fearless.

He is unstoppable when dealing with executives once he gets past a gatekeeper. He does not let a little thing like a gatekeeper stop him. Whether he is at an event where he meets a potential lead or is on the phone with a potential lead, he has an uncanny ability to relate to and connect with people of all levels.

The following is a sample of a script I would use once I am past the gatekeeper and have the executive on the phone. Let's call our executive Bob. Start off relating as if you already know and have a good rapport with the executive.

BOB: Hello?
ME: Hi Bob, it is Jennifer. How are you?
BOB: Hi Jennifer; I am sorry, what is this regarding?
ME: I had noticed we shared ABC Group on LinkedIn and thought you might be a great person to reach out to regarding X. I wanted to

connect with you and see if you had a minute to talk.

BOB: Well, I don't have much time to speak right now.

ME: No problem, I know you are extremely busy. I just noticed that you have XYZ need and wanted to connect with you to find out how I can be a resource for you.

This is one of the most valuable things I learned from one of the top networkers. Offer to be a resource! What I learned from him was that you should always find out how *you* can help *them*. Ask them what project they are most passionate about and/or how you can be a resource for them. Doing this creates camaraderie and shows them that you are not just interested in making it about you.

Another tip the speaker gave us was the 90/10 rule: Spend 90% of the time allowing the executive to talk and 10% of the time talking about yourself. If you follow those two principles, you will find a significant increase in your success rates.

## TAKE THE INITIATIVE TO SUCCEED

One of the most underutilized tools in becoming successful at what you do is to use the resources you already have available to you. To gather information in order to help my clients find top positions, I like to interview experts in their respective fields on what it was that has made them so successful.

I recently spoke with a very prosperous advertising sales representative for a national women's magazine, and she mentioned that one of the keys to her success was the research she did prior to landing her position. She knew that she wanted to get into an advertising sales position, and was committed to doing whatever it took to land her dream job. In order to prepare for what it was going to take for her to land her dream job, she began to have "informational" interviews with experts in her chosen field.

She approached key people in the industry she wanted to get into and proceeded to interview them on what it took for them to get to where they were. In doing so, she gained valuable information on what she herself would have to do if she wanted to flourish in her field.

Now, after twenty-five successful years as an advertising sales representative, she is thriving. You too can be a success in the field that most inspires you by simply applying the methods that those before you have already been successful with.

Do not let another day pass wherein you are doing something that does not fulfill you! Go out today, and find an individual in the field you are most interested in. Ask them if they will give you a few minutes of their time for an "informational" interview and you may be surprised by their answer.

## FAILURE IS NOT AN OPTION

Failure does not exist. There is only what works and what does not work. Edison said it best when he said, "I have not failed. I have just found 10,000 ways that won't work." When you redefine your definition of failure in a way that is empowering to you, you will be able to develop a new, more powerful relationship to your unfulfilled expectations. Remember, expectations are premade resentments.

For example, if you go to an interview where you prepared for hours rehearsing your answers over and over, yet you still get passed on, chances are you might wind up beating yourself up and thinking to yourself how unfair it is that you were not hired, or how you are not worth hiring. If instead you look at this as a learning opportunity you can create something very powerful. You could look at being passed on as a chance to grow yourself as an individual and as a potential employee. Take this opportunity to evaluate what was missing in the interview that might have made a difference and ask yourself "Would I have been happy in this job?" Often we sabotage an interview because we know intuitively the job is not what we want. Perhaps not being hired for that particular position is the best thing that could have happened. Look at what possibilities you can create out of NOT being the one who was chosen, and create an empowering context for your next interview.

Many people relate to failure as though failing means something is wrong with them. However, this perspective can be detrimental to one's personal growth and development, as well as to achieving one's goals.

Insanity has been defined as "Doing the same thing over and over again and expecting different results." If you find you keep getting the same results that do not work for you, then it is time for you to branch out and expand yourself in a whole new way. A great exercise that I suggest to job seekers is called the "Three NOs."

This exercise entails attempting to get three NOs from various people about something that is important to you. Your objective is to get the person you are asking to say NO. Some of you reading this might cringe at the thought of hearing NO, and others might think that getting a NO is not a big deal. Wherever you are at is perfect. The purpose of this exercise is to get present to your relationship to failure. By better understanding your relationship to failure and being able to be unstoppable in the face of hearing NO, you will learn to become fearless. A great example of practicing getting NOs is with dating.

If you are someone who is single, I encourage you to ask three complete strangers out on a date and be intentional in getting a NO from them. You might even be pleasantly surprised by a YES. The same goes for a job seeker. As a job seeker you can practice messaging CEOs and HR managers on LinkedIn and asking for an interview.

You might be surprised by the results you produce when you step forth boldly beyond your comfort level. It is in this moment that you will have access to being a stronger and unstoppable version of yourself.

# 4 | **The Resume**

*"The story of the human race is the story of men and women selling themselves short."*

Abraham Maslow

Your resume is, of course, the first thing a potential employer sees representing you. It must make a good impression—one strong enough to make a recruiter want to look at the rest of your information and striking enough to get attention in the very few seconds that are spent reading it. Employers rarely read past the first third of the first page (we get so many!), so it is important that they be immediately gripping. The rest of the resume must look great as well, and remember that your goal is to catch their attention enough that they *do* continue reading it and contact you!

## WHEN SHOULD I HAVE MY RESUME READY?

I often see people in this market who are unexpectedly laid off or terminated and therefore do not have a resume prepared. This can cost them valuable time in finding their next position. With the current economic condition, it is critical to strike while the iron is hot. If you see a position posted online that is a strong match for your background and you wait 24 hours to submit your resume because you do not have a resume and/or your resume is not up to date, you can lose out on that position.

My recommendation is that you always have an up-to-date resume, and that every time you get a new position you add that position to your existing resume. This is what I call your "master resume." Your master resume should have everything you have ever done listed on it and should be up to date at all times.

As different opportunities come up that you might be suitable for, you can adjust your master resume by adding or subtracting information to better suit the position you are applying for.

The easiest way to put your resume together is to utilize the "Resume Template" function in Microsoft Word. Resume Template offers hundreds of different templates for a variety of positions.

You never know what is going to happen in this economy, so no matter how secure you think your job is, make certain that your resume is in mint condition and ready to go at all times.

## GOOD FORMATTING

The most important thing in a resume is good formatting, followed by strong writing skills. If a resume is poorly formatted it will be dismissed no matter how well it is written. I typically delete any resumes that do not offer clean, easy-to-read formatting.

This means: "Summary of Qualifications" at the top. The Summary of Qualifications can be anywhere from two to five sentences that clearly depict why you are qualified for the position. Your "Work Experience" section should follow your Summary of Qualifications. Your Work Experience section should include strong action verbs and demonstrate how you can be of use to the company where you are applying.

It is important that you use bullets to draw the reader's attention and that your dates are lined up on the right-hand side of the page with your employer's name and your title on the left.

Finally, you want to have an "Education" and a "Skills" section. The Education portion should clearly list any degrees you have attained, but does not have to include the dates that you attained those degrees. The Skills section should list all of the relevant computer skills that you possess.

Avoid having a "hobby" or "interest" section; as for the most part employers do not care. If your hobbies and interests have led you to acquire relevant experience that would be valuable on the job, then include those with your experience in the appropriate section.

## BAD FORMATTING

There is no universal typesetting format that each resume has to follow. While that leaves a lot up to you as an applicant, it does not mean that it is a good idea to do anything to distract from what is important: why your background makes you the best candidate.

One of the most common errors I see on a resume is the inefficient use of page space. This will only make it seem as if you are intentionally leaving areas blank in order to cover up a lack of material. Think of the page space on your resume as valuable real estate. Every space on your resume should be used to make a case for why an employer should hire you, and should not be wasted. Be especially careful of having too wide of margins. Having wide margins can leave that valuable space unused!

Do not turn your resume into a narrative or use paragraph form when writing it. The resume needs to be an attractively presented

| SAMPLE ACTION VERBS TO USE IN YOUR RESUME | | | | |
|---|---|---|---|---|
| expedite | advise | analyze | approve | arrange |
| assemble | assist | build | collect | conceive |
| complete | conduct | control | coordinate | create |
| delegate | deliver | design | detect | develop |
| direct | discover | distribute | edit | eliminate |
| establish | evaluate | examine | expedite | formulate |
| generate | implement | improve | increase | influence |
| install | instruct | lead | maintain | manage |
| motivate | obtain | operate | order | organize |
| originate | oversee | participate | perform | plan |
| prepare | present | process | produce | program |
| promote | propose | protest | prove | provide |
| purchase | receive | recommend | record | reduce |
| reinforce | reorganize | represent | research | revamp |
| review | revise | schedule | select | sell |
| setup | test | train | write | |

collection of data that can be seen and understood at a glance so that you will get a call back from even the most inattentive and hurried recruiter. A story made up of paragraphs will almost certainly contain information you do not need, take too long to read and absorb, and will make you stand out in a bad way. Use a simple, conservative and information-rich format in assembling your resume.

Employers do not take the time to read your resume; they prefer to skim it. The same is true of lengthy paragraphs. In order to avoid an employer missing something important on your resume, use bullet points to highlight significant information and to break apart your resume more clearly.

Everything on your resume should be properly aligned, especially your dates and employers. I often come across resumes where nothing is aligned or some of the resume is aligned and then the rest is all over the place. This does not work! You need to make your resume visually appealing and easy to read. Setting proper alignment can help do this. When you do not properly align your dates and/or other important information on your resume, it can cause your resume to look sloppy. Take the time to set the necessary tabs to make everything line up appropriately and come across more clearly.

## SHOULD I USE A FUNCTIONAL OR REVERSE CHRONOLOGICAL RESUME?

When is it appropriate to use a functional vs. a reverse chronological resume?

First, let me start by explaining that a reverse chronological resume is what you see when you look at a typical resume. It starts with your most recent position and goes backwards with a description of each job. A functional resume is a list of all of your skills listed via bullet points at the top and a breakdown of your past employers listed at the bottom with simply your employer, title and dates and no description under each position.

So what type of resumes do employers prefer?

Hands down, recruiters and employers alike prefer reverse chronological resumes. The problem with functional resumes is that it is impossible to tell what type of work you did for each specific position. Interestingly, though, that is also the good thing about a functional resume format if you are looking to switch careers.

Functional resumes are good for three types of people:

1. Recent college graduates who do not have much work experience

2. People who are looking to transition out of one field into another

3. People who have a lot of movement on their resumes

Even though employers strongly dislike functional resumes, they are useful for recent college graduates. When you have recently graduated, you often do not have specific work experience; however, you do have skills that you acquired during school that you can list on your resume using the functional style.

The same is true for people who are changing careers. You might not have specific work experience in your target field, but you may have similar knowledge from your past position that you can list under your "Accomplishments" or "Summary of Qualifications" at the top of your functional resume.

As for people who have movement on their resumes (i.e., switching jobs every one to two years), functional resumes can be a good way to cover ten years of experience where you might have had seven to ten jobs. If you are someone who has a lot of movement on your resume, the best thing you can do is try to get a good position and stay there for at least four to seven years to get some stability on your resume.

In general, unless you are a recent college graduate or changing professions, I strongly recommend using a reverse chronological style resume.

## THE TOP TEN RESUME MISTAKES

Even if your resume is eye-catching, polished, complete and well written, it is important to remember that it can be undermined in an instant by an easy-to-overlook mistake. I have assembled some of the most dangerous resume traps out there—mistakes that anyone could make but which can sink an otherwise good resume instantly. They are certainly easy enough to make—I know because they are the mistakes I see time and time again from all varieties of job seekers. Read carefully so you know what to avoid!

### Not being 100% honest

Linda thinks that she has found her dream job. Her preliminary interviewers all seem to like her, and every reference says she does great work. But one day she suddenly finds herself out of the running. It turns out that the paralegal certificate from UCLA that she listed on her resume did not check out with UCLA, and when she was asked to produce it, it had the wrong Dean's name on it for the year she graduated. Linda tries to make the point that the job does not even require a paralegal certification, but that only makes her now-former potential employer wonder all the more why she would see the need to forge one.

If you cannot get a job by telling the truth, it is not a job you should be going for.

It can be tempting to lie on a resume in order to make yourself look better—or even to fudge dates when you cannot quite remember if you were hired in July or August of last year. There just are not any situations where the risk is worth it. Employers do check on the accuracy of the information they get in resumes, and if anything has been even slightly misrepresented, it is a good reason for them to dismiss the possibility of hiring you entirely. Even if something slips by and you are hired after submitting an inaccurate resume, there is actually a strong chance that you will be fired immediately when the truth comes out.

Present everything in the most flattering manner possible, but not to the point of deviating from verifiable facts. If you cannot be sure when you were hired for that old job, it is better just to give the month and year or just the year than to make up a specific date and run the risk of being proven wrong.

Even if you think that there is no way whoever reads your resume could check on a particular fact or if you think people will back you up when asked to verify what you say, you run a risk that is too great if it is a job you care about. I know one job seeker with a lawyer listed on her references who was willing to lie for her about how long she'd had her previous job. This lie worked fine—until prospective employers tried calling the office where she said she had been working, and they said she had not worked there for over five years. She was immediately dropped as a candidate.

We recruiters do have a "blacklist" of people coded DNU for "do not use." It is not especially easy to get on this list, but one of the best ways is to be caught falsifying your qualifications or employment history.

## Too much information/too many pages
After grabbing the reader's attention in just a few seconds, the resume has to be just deep enough to make the reader contact you for an interview, but not so complex that there is an overload of information.

There may be a lot that you want recruiters to know about you, but by and large, when they see a novel-length packet dropped on their desk, they will not go through the effort of reading seven pages before they find out what you can do for them. If too much information is listed, it becomes more difficult for the reader to discern the strengths and gems on your resume.

A perfect example of this was a man who sent his resume in for a plaintiff litigation paralegal position that I had posted. I had received close to a hundred resume submissions for this particular job posting and only had time to skim the first page of his four-page resume. When I did not see any relevant experience for the position on the first page of the resume, I quickly deleted it. The next day I got a call from him, irate that he had not heard back regarding his submission. I went through my deleted resume file and pulled up his resume, wherein I found that his "relevant" experience was not listed until the third page of his resume. Needless to say, he did not get the interview for that position and he has since rewritten his resume to be only one page.

Just as each candidate's work experience and work goals are different, each candidate's resume is going to be different as well. There is a balance that has to be struck between not enough information and too much, but a good rule of thumb for resume writing is to keep everything to under one page. Not only can you almost always fit everything that you need into that amount of space, but also a recruiter reviewing many people's resumes quickly is unfortunately not likely to investigate past a first page anyway. Do not let this make you feel too limited, though: the one-page guideline is actually helpful in that it should encourage you to boil your presentation down to just the most impressive and relevant elements.

Another good rule of thumb for those with longer work histories is that in general a resume should not go back longer than about ten years. What you want to get across is who you are now; information older than ten years will not usually be relevant. One exception to consider is that if you have over ten years of history with one company, you may want to break the rules and run on to the second page; you want to show what you learned with your long-time employer, but you also want to show yourself having more than one job if possible.

Sylvia is a candidate for a job posting in an area where she has extensive experience. She creates a short resume that highlights the relevance of the experience that she has, but when she submits it, employers pass on it nonetheless when they see that in order to pad it out, Sylvia has listed "retail therapy" among her hobbies.

Most of the time, hobbies have no place in a serious resume, unless they provide relevant real-world experience to the job you are looking for (if you are applying to work as an entertainment critic, your movie-reviews blog certainly has a place). But a line like "retail therapy" can only hurt rather than help.

As an obvious joke, it shows the reader of the resume that the applicant is not taking the process seriously. A sense of humor is seen as a good quality, but a mistimed, bad or offensive joke can do far more damage than a good one—and even the world's greatest comedians cannot manage to get a laugh on every line. A good rule of thumb to keep in mind is that the people who usually think they "have a sense of humor" are those who laugh at our jokes, rather than the ones who make us laugh the most. The pressure to be ready to laugh at the boss's weak jokes is the stuff of cliché—but it is usually also good policy.

Before even thinking about including a less-than-relevant hobby or a frivolous comment, think first about what it reflects on you. Does it show you as someone who can put the interests of the business first? Would a company that wants a person to handle books and finances be confident in someone who practices "retail therapy?"

## Personal baggage

All that your potential employer needs to know from your resume is why they need to hire you. Any extra information about other subjects is too much. Do not list why you left your last job; even if you have the best of all possible reasons for leaving, listing a reason can only hurt your chances and cannot help them. It is occasionally advisable to include your reasons for leaving in a cover letter, but only when the employer might have serious reservations about why you have moved around so much.

Do not list your salary at previous jobs on your resume. It does not bear on your new one, and cannot help you at all—a lower salary can make you seem less skilled or make your new employer want to pay you less, and a higher one can make them expect you will demand too much or not stay too long in the position. Only list your prior salary history if instructed to do so on the application. Otherwise, leave it blank and negotiate salary later (more on that coming!).

Do no list unrelated hobbies or "filler" material; that will only make you seem *less* qualified than you would be if you had left it off.

## Photos, fonts and borders

Sorry if you feel like I am stifling your creativity, but, again, the resume is there only as a source of information. Anything that does not transmit information about you that is relevant to the job you are applying for has got to go, including images, colorful borders or fancy text-art fonts that take up valuable space that can be used for content. This will almost always be perceived as gaudy and tacky at best, or as an intentional screen for a lack of content.

Use a conservative font. Print in black and use italics or underlines for emphasis only sparingly. Wild typography is very distracting, and gives the reader the impression that you are trying to cover up for lightness on substance. I see this often, and every time it is the person who submits a professional, black-and-white resume that lets the words themselves do the talking who ends up looking better than one who submits a resume with less clear typography.

## Far away address

There are plenty of reasons you may want to list an address on your resume far from the job where you are applying. Perhaps you are in the process of moving, or maybe you are intending to move if you get the position. Unfortunately, the fact is that this can make employers less likely to hire you, thinking that it is not necessarily worth the effort of bringing you on board if your distance might make you refuse the offer anyway. If a company can hire someone just as qualified as you, but the other person lives locally, chances are they will choose the person who lives closer rather than risk dealing with relocation costs and the chance that you might decide not to relocate after all.

It is also important to be careful about posting your resume on www. monster.com or www.careerbuilder.com with your home address. You never know who might find that information. For those candidates that do want to list their address or need to list their address for particular jobs, I always recommend getting a PO Box during the time that you are looking. Getting a PO Box can be a good way to avoid any unwanted solicitations. If you live out of area, you may want to consider leaving your address off your resume, getting a PO Box in the area you are relocating to, or finding out if you can use a friend's address in the area you are looking to move to.

There is no right answer, but if you notice you are not getting interviews in locations that are further away, you may want to consider alternative options.

## Inappropriate contact information

Many of us set up our first email addresses years ago, and the chances are pretty good that we chose a username that was possibly a little goofy and designed to impress our friends. In this case, it is time to put away childish things and get a businesslike, frivolity-free email address. Even the best of resumes will fail to impress even the most desperate of employers if it asks them to contact you at an email address such as sexylegs69@yahoo.com. Email services such as Gmail, Yahoo! Mail, and Hotmail (to name only the most popular) are free, so there is no reason not to get a new email for professional purposes. Use some permutation of your real name: if you're called John William Baker, then you are likely to find jbaker, jwbaker, johnwbaker, etc., taken, but—boring as it may seem—being johnbaker6532086 is infinitely better than asking potential employers to email you as "slacker420."

## Phone number

It is hard to make a phone number look unprofessional, but things can be just as bad when employers try to dial it:

> Frank has an excellent resume, and submitted it with a
> well-written cover. A human resources manager's eye was

caught, and she was impressed upon reading the resume. She decides to give Frank a call and set up an interview, but he was in the shower when she called and could not pick up the phone. However, she decided not to leave a message or to call him back when she heard a voicemail message that incorporated profanity-laced clips from a Kanye West song.

Once again, every point of contact you have with a prospective employer is essentially a part of the interview. If you would not sit down with your interviewer and start performing your favorite rapper's most violent or sexual lyrics, do not leave them on your voicemail message for that same interviewer to hear. Songs, gag messages and most messages containing anything other than your name, phone number, and a request that you leave a message may make your friends laugh, but it is worth your time and effort to change them to something more professional when you are expecting business calls.

On the other side of the coin, make sure not to be so impersonal that you leave the default answering machine in effect, with a computerized voice reading off your number. Business callers will want to be sure that they reached the right person and to know that you took the care to record a businesslike message.

Any point of contact with a potential employer is important when you are looking for a job; whether or not you give a professional impression can win or lose you the opportunity, even if it happens when an interviewer calls your phone and you are not there.

## Personal pronouns

Yes, your resume should be all about you. But it should not read like a long personal narrative or diary entry. Including sentences like "I worked for Businessco Incorporated. I overhauled their computer system. I made great improvements in its operation" sounds amateurish and manages to turn what could be an impressive accomplishment into something that seems like a boast. Keep in mind that employers are looking for a resume that feels like an objective list of achievements, experience and qualifications—not a personal statement.

## Vagueness and generic statements

Most people have some area of their resume that they would rather gloss over quickly rather than explain in detail if given the opportunity. However, the way to handle these spots is not to sweep them under the rug, but rather to spin them as much as possible into assets. A lot of applicants leave sections general and vague in the hope that it will help hide weak areas or cover more ground. In fact, it does the opposite.

Do not just write that you have "experience using business software applications," but explain which ones you have used and what you have done with them. Do not just say you "worked in the marketing department," but explain what your responsibilities were. If you had a period when you were not working, think about what you were doing during that time that could apply to the jobs you are applying for now.

Using a generic statement, such as "customer oriented," without backing that statement up with a result can hurt your resume. Anyone can say they are "customer oriented," but unless they can back that statement up with evidence to support it, those are just words. Instead of using a generic statement such as "customer oriented," use a specific example that illustrates how customer oriented you are, for example, "Achieved 100% customer satisfaction over a six-month period by listening to and understanding customer's needs."

Your resume is no place for modesty. If a part of your background is important enough to recommend you on a resume, include it in as much detail as you have space for. If not, leave it out.

## Grammar and spelling errors

Nobody makes these on purpose, but they slip by in everyone's writing. Even small typos in a business document such as a resume can severely hurt your chances. It is often hardest to notice one's own errors, so it is never a bad idea to have somebody else take a look at your resume and check it for accuracy before you send it along.

## OBJECTIVES

A lot of people consider it standard to include a section of "objectives" on a resume, where the applicant lists his or her goals in applying for the job. For the most part, though, it is pretty obvious what your objective is in applying: You want the job. Since that is usually quite clear, the "objectives" section often gets populated by filler that does say much and distracts from the rest of the resume.

There are only two reasons, in my opinion, to have an objective listed on your resume.

1. If you are a student with little to no work experience in a particular field, then it is appropriate to add an objective so that the potential employer can see what type of job you are interested in.

2. If you are changing to a new career after already having worked in a different field. In this case it is helpful to identify what new industry you are pursuing (if it is not already clear from the resume).

I personally think objectives are an outdated tool, and should be replaced with a "Summary of Qualifications" or nothing at all. If it is already apparent from your resume what your end goal is in a position, then repeating the information in an objective or "Summary of Qualifications" can be redundant.

If you are going to use the "Summary of Qualifications," you should keep it short and to the point. There is no need to provide more than three to four sentences. Also, be sure not to repeat information in your "Summary of Qualifications" that is already listed in other areas on your resume, otherwise you are just wasting page space. If a resume is done well, it should be clear to the employer what your objective is without having to state your objective outright.

## REFERENCES

References will be an important part of the hiring process for your potential employer, but you do not need to take up valuable space on your resume by listing them. Have them at the ready, though, and indicate a willingness on the resume to provide them. It is always a good idea to have at least three to five references available when applying; at least two of these should be supervisor references. Preferably, these should be from different companies and/or positions and should be from the past five to ten years.

Employers like to see that the references they are checking are not simply from your friends at work or from coworkers who never had the opportunity to work with you closely. Getting references from supervisors who have had the opportunity to oversee your work and know your relationships within the company is a good way for them to do this.

In the business world it is expected that employees will ask their coworkers and superiors for references (and many people will actually be flattered by the request), so there is no reason to avoid being straight-forward with your requests. Knowing that your new employer will want to speak with important or supervisory figures can help you tailor your references to give them the best possible impression. Choose the people you have the best chance of getting not just a complimentary but also a detailed and specific reference from.

### Proper reference etiquette

An employer or recruiter who is checking a reference is looking for three key components:

1. What the reference says in response to the questions about you.

2. The tone with which the reference talks about their experience working with you.

3. The length of the answer that reference gives in response to a question.

Part of being a recruiter or HR person is being able to understand what is not said during a reference. If an employer gives us short, one-word answers in response to the questions we ask or uses a negative tone, that response typically gives us pause. It is not always a deal-breaker if the answers are short or the tone is not that enthusiastic; however, we do take all things into consideration when checking references.

The best potential references to select to give to an employer or recruiter are those people who directly supervised your work. Recruit-ers and employers for the most part are not interested in talking to peers or personal acquaintances. Once you have chosen the people whose names you are going to give out, it is critical to personally speak with each person before a potential employer calls to check your reference. Additionally, references typically speak more highly of those people with whom they have regularly kept in touch.

Finally, it is important *not* to list your references on your resume. It is appropriate to have a separate list of your references and to only provide that list once requested by the employer or recruiter. Otherwise, if you include your references on your resume they might be abused by people you do not want calling them.

## DEGREE OR NOT DEGREE?

In today's market, it is more important than ever to be careful of what you put on your resume and how you word it. One of the biggest errors I see repeatedly occurs when people list a college degree or certificate on their resume—but they have not completed the classes necessary to possess that degree or certificate. Additionally, I see people who call themselves "certified," but they do not seem to understand what that term means. Neither of these is acceptable and can be grounds for a rescinded job offer and/or termination. This is not always done intentionally; however, it can be done as a way to defraud a potential employer.

The following are a few rules to follow when it comes to listing or not listing degrees, certificates or college units on your resume.

1. Unless you have completed all of the courses necessary for a particular degree or certificate, do not list it on your resume. Listing units that you have completed on your resume can just complicate things and can lead to confusion.

   *Example:* "Attended Cornell University."

   This is not clear as to whether you received a degree and can complicate things.

2. Do not list a degree or certificate on your resume if it is NOT required for that job. For the most part, when you add a degree or certificate to your resume that is not a requirement for the position, you are making the employer's life harder by giving them one more thing to verify and/or giving them one more reason not to hire you if everything does not check out perfectly.

Lucy has what appears to be an excellent resume. She has longevity at her most recent company, and she has a bachelor's degree listed as well. The employer immediately responds to her resume and brings her in for an interview. Everyone loves Lucy and they make her an offer contingent upon successful completion of a background check. During the background check, however, it comes back that they are unable to verify her bachelor's degree. When the recruiter calls to clarify if she does have her bachelor's degree, Lucy explains that she "has two associate degrees, which she thought counted as a bachelor's degree." The company was unable to move forward with hiring her even though they loved her and thought that she had great skills.

The only time you should list a degree if it is not required for the job is if you have a JD. You have to be careful about not listing a JD on your resume, as there can be certain legalities a company has to comply with if you have passed the bar or possess a JD and are employed with that company.

3. It is critical that you *never* list a degree or certificate on your resume unless you can provide an authentic copy of that degree or certificate.

4. Do not list dates of your degree or certificate on your resume as this can cause people to guess your age and discriminate against you, and/or if you are off by a month or a year and the degree or certificate is verified for a different time period then what you have listed, this can also cause an offer to be rescinded.

## WHERE CAN I GET RESUME TEMPLATES?

Why reinvent the wheel when there are thousands of resume templates out there to choose from? One of my favorite suggestions for creating a new resume is to use the resume templates available in Microsoft Word. The template is very easy to use. Just follow the instructions as shown in the figures and you will have automatic access to hundreds of free resume templates for a variety of professions.

Once you have the template, fill in the blanks and style it to make it your own. Additionally, I suggest adding your LinkedIn URL if you have one. It is important to have your resume proofread by at least one or two other people. You can pay someone hundreds or even thousands of dollars to revise it for you, but I highly encourage you to give it a try on your own first so that way it truly expresses who you are to an employer and saves you money!

## SAMPLE REVERSE CHRONOLOGICAL RESUME

**Name**                          LinkedIn URL
Address                           email address
Phone Number

### SUMMARY OF QUALIFICATIONS

Experienced . . .

### EXPERIENCE

***Company Month/Year–Present***
*Title*
- ACTION VERB FOLLOWED BY RESULT YOU PRODUCED
- Generated over $100,000 in temporary staffing business in 2011.
- Fostered and maintained long-term relationships with key clients regarding their staffing needs.

***Company Month/Year–Month/Year***
*Title*
- Increased personal sales from $370k to $527k in less than one year.
- Revolutionized recruiting practices within the firm by establishing an innovative candidate coaching system that resulted in an average Send Out to Placement ratio of less than 4:1.
- Created a successful niche from scratch in the area of real estate, including over 100k in revenue in less than one year from the world's largest retail property group.
- Utilized resources such as www.linkedin.com, www.careerbuilder.com, and other similar websites to recruit and network with candidates for various job requisitions.
- Attended various conferences and hiring fairs to direct recruit and source candidates for various positions.
- Managed and worked within a candidate database of over 30,000 candidates to enhance my recruiting efforts.
- Achieved high retention rate from year to year for all candidates placed.

### EDUCATION

*BA Degree*

### SKILLS

Microsoft Word, Excel and PowerPoint

## SAMPLE FUNCTIONAL RESUME FROM MICROSOFT WORD

[email] ▪ Ext: [phone]

# [YOUR NAME]

### Accomplishments

- Eight years of editorial experience in the area of print and online technical communication.
- Appointed chief coordinator on the A. Datum Corporation Editorial Board.
- Developed, researched, and delivered on time the A. Datum Corporation Style Guide.
- Wrote specifications for the Editorial Request Tool, an innovative design using Microsoft Visual Basic to enable the efficient submission of requests to the A. Datum Corporation Editorial Board.
- For more than four years, managed the editorial department at Consolidated Messenger, which consisted of four employees who provided editorial coverage to the company's then 21 writers.

### Professional Experience

**Technical Editor III–A. Datum Corporation, [City, ST] ▪ [Month, Year] – Present**

- Develop and publish editorial procedures to support the more than 80 writers who document peer-to-peer services and network strategies in the e-commerce space.
- Specify and prototype tools to increase editorial efficiently in the workplace, and work directly with writing teams to develop customer-focused content.
- Edited content, managed four editors, and provided usability feedback for website development projects that showcased the company's business-to-business wireless services.

**Projects Editor–Litware, Inc., [City, ST] ▪ [Month, Year] – [Month, Year]**

- Researched, wrote, and edited content for the department's website. Conducted usability studies on the site and provided troubleshooting assistance as needed.

**Freelance Writer–<u>Baldwin Museum of Science</u>, [City, ST]** • **[Month, Year] – [Month, Year]**
- Interviewed specialists in scientific areas and wrote informative articles on current scientific practices and theory as they pertained to the mission of the museum.
- Purchased articles were printed in the quarterly 32-page magazine published by the museum.
- Wrote and edited feature news articles and press releases for daily metropolitan newspaper under stringent deadlines. Highlights include covering the North Carolina Incident.

**Programming and Software Skills**
Microsoft Visual Basic, HTML, Microsoft Office, Microsoft Windows, Adobe PhotoShop and Illustrator

**Education**
- [Degree Obtained] – [College Name], [City, ST] • [Year]

## TINKERING

The high importance of a resume means that many job seekers feel compelled to tinker with theirs eternally, changing font sizes and the order of their accomplishments until the cows come home—and never actually applying for any jobs. The reality is that you do not need to do this.

Your resume's only purpose is to get you the interview, which then gets you the job. It will never do this if it sits around unsent. Get your resume to a point where you are satisfied with it, then **stop**. Endless revision can be a paralyzing cycle that stops you from ever putting your foot out and applying. Once you are at a reasonably satisfactory point, it makes sense to spend your energy on sending it to employers rather than on going back and making frequent changes. You should only have to do this if the resume as it stands is not working for you.

If you send out ten resumes and get three or more responses, then leave your resume alone. The only purpose of having a resume is to get you interviews. Consider the fact that in the field of direct mail (or what you and I might less charitably refer to as junk mail), a 1% success rate is considered fantastically successful. We tend to expect resumes to do a little better than junk mail letters, but as long as you are steadily generating an appreciable stream of positive responses—then let well enough alone!

When I review a resume, I try to look for what the person is doing right, and point out their strengths. In addition, I look for ways they can enhance their resume through several critiques and modifications. However, not all people need to modify their resumes. In other words, if you are already getting responses from employers regarding your resume, DO NOT TOUCH IT. The only reason to revise and/or revamp your resume is if you are not getting the results you want, that is, your resume is not getting you interviews.

When you are getting interviews in the field you are interested in, you are already ahead of the game and should leave it as it is and put resume writing behind you. Getting in the door through your resume is only half the battle. When you have scored interviews, you then need to focus on your interviewing skills in order to make sure that you meet your ultimate goal of *getting the offer.*

## DOES IT MATTER WHO SENDS OUT YOUR RESUME?

Yes it does! It is extremely important that you know who sent your resume and when it was sent. One of the downfalls of working with numerous recruiters is that your resume can accidentally be sent to the same company twice. Some companies may disqualify you from the position if this happens as it makes you look unorganized.

It is important to keep meticulous track of where your resume has been sent, by whom it was sent and when it was sent. Many job seekers do not know this, but when a recruiter sends your resume to a company for a position, that recruiter typically has "ownership" of that resume for anywhere from six months to a year. This is why you want to be certain you always know who is sending your resume out, and that you only work with recruiters who are looking out for your best interests.

It can hurt your chances of getting a job if two different parties send your resume to the same company. This is why I recommend making sure that whether it is you or the recruiter that sends out a given resume, it is added with all the appropriate information to your spreadsheet so that you know who you have already applied to and when to follow up.

Keeping track of this information will help you to avoid confusion with the company and/or the agency you are working with and it will make you look like you are on top of your game. Both the company and the agency will appreciate it. It will also help you if you want to resubmit your resume for another position within the same company. If you have this information you can mention it in your cover letter that your resume was submitted for another position on XYZ date.

## FINAL DOS AND DON'TS

To wrap up and review, let's look at some of the biggest dos and don'ts of the resume-writing process. Everyone's resume will be different, but if you keep to these guidelines and remember the advice I have given you, yours should rise above the rest!

## DO:

1. Add your LinkedIn URL to your resume if you have a well-put-together LinkedIn profile and recommendations on your profile (which you should!).

2. Have a summary of what makes you qualified (remember—objectives are basically obsolete!) listed at the top of your resume.

3. Have a well-formatted resume with position title and company listed on the left, dates aligned on the right and experience bulleted.

4. List strong adverbs, such as *facilitated, managed, organized,* etc., followed by your accomplishments.

5. Spell-check your resume and have someone else look it over for grammatical, punctuation and/or formatting errors.

## DO NOT:

1. List your reference contact information on your resume.

2. Include a photo or any bizarre graphics (unless you are in graphic design or related field).

3. Use ALL CAPS or all *italics* to write your resume.

4. Lie about ANYTHING on your resume because it can all be verified.

5. Use different fonts and/or different sizes in the same sections. For example, if your section titles such as "Experience" or "Skills" are in size 18 Arial and bold, then that should be the same for every section head. The same goes for the font and size used for your bullet points.

## COVER LETTER

I am often asked what a good cover letter should look like, and whether cover letters are still relevant in today's market. First let me say that the old version of the cover letter, which was submitted separately from your resume as an addendum, has become obsolete. It is rare to have a company request or want to read an applicant's cover letter in addition to his or her resume. It is also unusual for an employer to ask for a faxed cover letter or resume, let alone a "snail mail" cover letter and resume. Some clients may request a writing sample, but this is not the same as a cover letter.

The cover letter of today is typically included in the body of the email you use to submit your resume. When sending an email cover letter to a potential employer with your resume attached, be sure that the cover letter/email is short and simple and that it encapsulates the themes that you want your resume to highlight. It helps to directly address any potential concerns, such as visible recent job instability or gaps in your employment history, that an employer might have.

The following is a sample that you can use as a reference when drafting a letter:

Dear Sir or Madam:

I am very interested in working with XXX in a XXX position. Enclosed is a copy of my resume for your consideration and review. I feel that my X and Y skills could be a tremendous asset to your company.

I have spent the last 10+ years as a Title Here in the xxx field. Though I thoroughly enjoyed my time in my last position, I am ready to pursue new horizons.

I am committed to contributing my expertise to XXX, while learning and developing new skills that will facilitate company growth and expansion. My combination of in-depth skilled training and practical experiences at various companies makes me a unique candidate to contribute to the efficiency of the organization. I pride myself on fostering a positive mental attitude both in myself and the team around me.

Should you have any additional questions about my background, please feel free to contact me. I look forward to meeting with you in person to discuss my qualifications and to discuss how I can be a resource for your team. Thank you for your time and consideration.

Sincerely,
Signature

# 5 | The Mental Side of Your Search

*"Watch your thoughts for they become words. Watch your words for they become actions. Watch your actions for they become habits. Watch your habits for they become your character. And watch your character for it becomes your destiny. What we think, we become. My father always said that . . . and I think I am fine."*

Margaret Thatcher

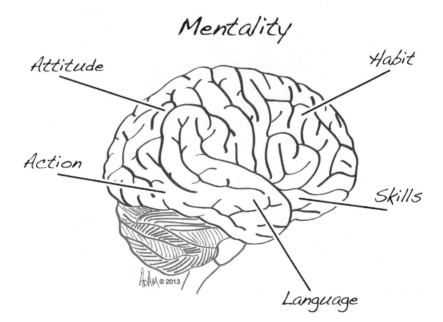

## WHAT YOU SAY IS WHAT YOU GET

Have you ever listened to what people say? I mean, really listened? Over the last few years I have begun to pay attention to the language that people use in their job hunt and how it directly correlates to their effectiveness or lack of it in finding a job.

What I have begun to notice is that people who consistently use disempowering and passive language such as "I hope," "I'll try," "I might," "Maybe" or "One day" tend to be less effective in obtaining the jobs they want than those who use more affirmative and empowering language such as "I will," "I can," "I intend," "I am creating," etc.

Though I am not a neuropsychologist, I love the study of the brain and understanding how and why we do what we do. I believe the language we use has a direct relationship to our ability to attain our goals. I have personally played with this theory over the past ten years and have found that using empowering and affirmative language does have a direct correlation on my effectiveness, as well as on the effectiveness of those I have taught these principles to.

One of the first things that I teach job seekers who come into my office is how to use affirmative and empowering language in their job search. Essentially, I tell them to start noticing the words they use to describe their job search and to omit the words that are disempowering.

This is also true of negatively discussing your job search with others. The most common phrase I hear used by unemployed job seekers is "It is hard." It is hard, meaning their job search. When you begin replacing "It is hard" with things like "I am getting out there" and/or "I am making progress," you will start to notice that different results will begin to appear. Often these results are getting you closer to the job you really want.

In a class I lead called "Making Yourself Indispensable in the Workplace," I coach job seekers to keep a notepad with them and to write down every time they complain during one full day. From there, I teach them to notice the impact their complaints have on those around them. What I have found is that many of us do not even realize how often we complain and how our complaints begin to create our reality. When we replace our complaints with proactive or positive language about what is working, rather than what is not working, our perspective begins to change as well. Once your perspective begins to alter, your attitude, beliefs and actions will slowly alter as well to be in line with your new perspective on what you are committed to.

One of the best quotes that I have heard is "If you want to know what you are committed to, look at what you have."

This statement can be biting for some people, because they do not want to take responsibility for the circumstances in their lives. When you begin to take responsibility for both the good and the bad things that happen in your life, you are no longer the victim of your life; you are the cause of it and you will begin to have power over the direction your life goes.

## ARE YOU READY TO MAKE YOUR MOVE?

Considering that you have made it this far, I am going to take it as a resounding "YES!" that you are ready to make your next career move and/or find your next position. As I stated earlier, one of the most important aspects of the job hunt that is often overlooked is the mental aspect. Your perspective and attitude are just as important as how strong your resume is or what you do or do not say in an interview. That said, how can you mentally prepare yourself to make that big career transition or overcome the unemployment blues?

You can begin to shift the way you think and feel by shifting your perspective. Just as I worked with Sue on her Statement of Intent and Daily Declaration, so too can you begin to shift your perspective by creating your own Statement of Intent and Daily Declaration.

These terms may be entirely new to you or you may have heard of something similar in books such as "The Secret" and "Think and Grow Rich" (both of which I highly recommend!). The specific concepts of a Daily Declaration and Statement of Intent are something that I created several years ago.

The first time I used my Daily Declaration and Statement of Intent was when I wanted to make over $100,000 a year. I was a junior recruiter and was in my early 20's. At the time $100,000 seemed like an insurmountable amount of money to make. I could not have fathomed making that much money in three years, let alone making that amount of money in one year. At that point, I had taken a lot of knowledge from the books I mentioned earlier, as well as from a class that I had taken called Landmark Education, and combined them to come up with the ideas of a Statement of Intent and Daily Declaration.

My first Statement of Intent it was focused solely on money; however, I have since expanded my Statement of Intent to create a wide variety of things, including booking television shows, creating business and much more. The key components to creating an effective Statement of Intent are "WHAT," that is, what you want to accomplish; "WHEN," by when you want to accomplish it; and last but most importantly, you must be SPECIFIC! Statements of Intent that are not specific will get you nowhere fast (example: I want a great job). It is also important to use only affirmative and empowering language as discussed earlier. Creating a Statement of Intent will give you an opportunity to take "hope" out of it, replacing words like "hope" and "try" with words such as "create" and "intend."

An example of what your Statement of Intent could look like would be something like this:

"By December 31, 2013 (WHEN—typically I recommend picking a date three months to one year out so that you have enough time to retrain your brain and to accomplish what you intend), I will have a position paying me $60,000 or more (always add "or more" when speaking about things you are looking for more of, such as money) that is within ten miles of my house and where I get to work in an environment where I look forward to going to work every day (YES! Do be that specific—it goes back to that old adage, be careful what you wish for because you might just get it!)."

Once you have your Statement of Intent, keep it where it is easy to get to so that you can declare it out loud a minimum of once a day, and ideally two to three times a day (you can keep it next to your bed, in your bathroom and/or on your iPhone). When I first started doing my Daily Declaration (your Statement of Intent said out loud), I would say it every morning before I got out of bed. At first my boyfriend (now husband) was annoyed, but by the second year of doing it (and making well over six figures) he was cheering me on!

The reason it is important to turn your Statement of Intent into a Daily Declaration is that your brain and subconscious will sabotage you at first and hold you back from getting what you want. Once you begin declaring your Statement of Intent out loud every day, you will begin to notice that you take actions in line with your Statement of Intent, and it will also help retrain your brain to be in line with your new goals.

Many people will write out a goal or intention, but few will take the time to declare it. What I am suggesting is not something new or innovative. These concepts have been around for thousands of years and these same concepts are what have made successful men and women around the world able to achieve their highest goals, financial and otherwise. The concept of the Statement of Intent and the Daily Declaration are just my way of saying it.

Over the past ten years, I have taught thousands of people to be effective using these easy methods. Even if you don't believe me, try it! What is the worst that could happen? You might actually wind up with the results you want and have to confront your own power and success! At the end of the day, we are the only ones responsible for our lives and our futures (the good and the bad). Once you take ownership of how your life turns out, you will never again be a victim of your circumstances and can begin to create the life that you have always dreamed was possible.

## SKILLS VS. ATTITUDE

I have noticed as a recruiter is that the better someone's attitude is, the more likely it is that they are to be hired. Noticing this, I surveyed numerous human resources professionals who hire job seekers through me (both temporary and permanent) about whether they would prefer someone with stronger skills or a better attitude and they unanimously answered that attitude trumps skills.

What does attitude mean? What my clients mean by having a good attitude is the following:

1. Always be willing to pitch in and help out your peers or your bosses.

2. Never complain or gossip.

3. Have a pleasant demeanor; including smiling and being upbeat about things, especially when there is a problem or challenge.

4. No task is too big or too small for you to handle.

5. Never leave someone hanging on a project or assignment (i.e., not following through).

If you focus on these five areas, your attitude will automatically improve and both employers and others will gravitate towards you and want to hire you.

Skills do play an important role in some positions, but it is your skills multiplied by your attitude that gets you and keeps you the job.

*(Good Skills)* × *(Good Attitude)* = *Employment*

If you do not have a *can do* attitude you cannot get the job, or if you do get the job, you eventually will be terminated.

What does this mean? Your attitude about your job search and your current situation can directly impact how effective you are in finding a new position. Numerous talented individuals are in the job market right now, and yes, it is very competitive. This, however, does not mean it is impossible to find a wonderful job. Job seekers are being hired every day, and often into great positions. So you may be wondering what is it that they have that you do not. They have a positive mental attitude and perseverance. Many of these job seekers may have also been looking for a job for months or years, but this did not hinder them in finding that perfect position. They worked every day on finding a positive outlook and eventually, their positive attitude got them hired.

## KNOW THE KEYS TO SUCCESS

*"I would rather die of passion than of boredom."*

*Vincent van Gogh*

We all have different goals, so when we succeed we all succeed in different ways. But that certainly does not mean that there are not extremely important common denominators to pick out. In fact, business success almost always boils down to one simple equation that you need to keep in mind: success = passion + perseverance.

Think about it for a moment and you will find that one without the other never leads very far, and true success rarely arrives without a healthy supply of both. The people in life who are most successful and can sustain their success are those who are passionate about what they do. If you are not passionate about what you do, how will you be able to sustain your success long term? It seems like every one of the successful people I've interviewed loves getting out of bed every day. Is that true of you? When you love what you do, other people can tell, and the monetary rewards will quickly follow.

But passion alone will not help you to be a success in your chosen field. You must also have the drive and the willingness to persevere as a complement to your passion. Without drive your passion will never amount to much. You can be tremendously passionate and excited about a certain product or service—but until you back that passion with ambition and perseverance you will not go far. Ambition is necessary because you need to be unstoppable in achieving your goals when things do not go your way. Many of the successful people whom I have interviewed went through hard times and had to persevere in the face of their hardships. Some immediately attained success, but even their success could not have been sustained long term without a driving force that has them continue to do what they know they need to do to be successful.

So if you are looking to be a success in your field, ask yourself: What am I passionate about? Then go out there and start to do it. In addition, set goals for yourself, and go after them. Do not get deterred when things do not go your way. You must persevere to achieve your dreams!

## RELIABLE—MAKE YOURSELF WHAT YOU WANT TO BE

*"It is not only what we do, but also what we do not do, for which we are accountable."*

*Moliere*

Any company wants to hire somebody with integrity—a person who could be described as reliable. And the number one way to convince an employer that you are reliable is to live what you want to seem—actually be reliable.

Are you someone that others can count on to show up? Are you someone who is accountable for your actions? Are there areas in your life that you are responsible for, but others that you let slide by? Why is it that we always place blame, rather than take responsibility?

If you have done any of the following five things in the last 60 days, I would encourage you to ask yourself: How responsible am I?

1. Been late for an appointment or meeting.
2. Not shown up for an event or commitment without calling to let anyone know.
3. Cancelled plans with less than 24 hours' notice.
4. Missed a deadline for a project.
5. Paid a bill late.

If you have missed a deadline or appointment it does not make you a bad person. Everyone has to cancel an appointment or push back a deadline from time to time. Simply use this to become aware of how your actions directly relate to other people's perception of you. If you are someone who is consistently late, or does not show up, chances are you might be viewed as someone who is unreliable or flaky. Being an individual who others can rely on is of the utmost importance in your business and professional life. In order to have success both in life and in one's career, others must be able to trust you and to know that they can count on you to keep your word. Every time you break a promise others lose a little more faith in you, until one day they no longer feel they can rely on you at all.

Following are the top three steps that you can take to transform your relationship to responsibility:

1. Do a personal assessment of where you are breaking your word and get in communication with those you have broken your word with.
2. Get present to the fact that every action you take has an effect on those around you.
3. Practice saying "No." Only commit to things that you can accomplish so that you will set realistic expectations for yourself and for others.

Taking responsibility for yourself and your actions is the first step towards personal and professional success.

## DEFENSIVENESS + UNACCOUNTABILITY = UNEMPLOYMENT

A big complaint that I have heard repeatedly from clients regarding both temporary and full-time employees is that employees are being defensive and/or not taking responsibility for their actions. I often hear clients say that someone is "combative" and does not respond well to criticism or feedback. The other item I have been hearing about is that employees are full of excuses as to why it will not or cannot work or why they cannot do it.

This sort of "negative Nancy" attitude where employees are constantly refusing to do work, questioning the work they are asked to do and/or complaining about the work they are given is setting them up for failure and/or termination.

So how do you prevent yourself from becoming one of the people who an employer is considering letting go of or terminating?

A few things that you can work on to avoid being let go because of a bad attitude include:

- Look at any potential insecurities you might have in a particular area and figure out a way to enhance that area. For example, if you don't have strong Microsoft Word skills, go out and get training to enhance your skills.

- Do not give excuses when asked why something was not done. Just apologize and figure out a way to DO IT.

- If you have a question or something you do not understand, be in communication immediately about any questions you may have regarding a particular task or duty.

- When being given criticism or feedback regarding your performance, be accountable. Take responsibility for your actions without complaining, deflecting or being defensive.

## HABITS

A few years ago, I had the opportunity to interview a CEO of a multimillion dollar company. He began his career as a CPA, and taught himself how to be successful and run a business. There are three things to which he attributes his success, and that he explained are absolutely necessary to being rewarded monetarily in the business world. These three attributes are the following:

1. Timeliness
2. Accuracy
3. Economics

An old business adage says that you can often attain two of the above traits but rarely can find all three. When someone possesses all three of these distinctions and applies them in the working world, they will always be the ones who are rewarded. It goes back to the old saying of, "Doing more than you are paid for." If you are hired for a particular position, and consistently produce accurate work, before the deadline and profitably, you will be rewarded!

Keep these attributes in mind. You want to convince employers that they are advantages that *you* have, so play up examples of them in communications with your potential employers. As they are essential characteristics for business success, it is not without reason that employers are looking for them—so make all three of them into habits as consistently as you can. They will be as helpful to you in getting the job as they will to help you to thrive and advance once you have it.

## KNOW YOURSELF . . . AND BE PROUD!

One of the many hindrances for job seekers in landing the job of their dreams is not acknowledging themselves for all of the things that make them amazing. Many of us are taught as children that we should not boast or be proud. While you certainly may not want to be the type of person who only cares about him or herself, you also do not want to downplay your greatness and what you have to contribute to the world.

In business, realizing your own greatness—that which differentiates you from others in a positive way—can often result in landing your dream job. In interviewing people who are successful in their field, I find that they have all concurred that having confidence in oneself is vital to being successful in business and in life. You are doing the world no favors by holding your greatness back. I invite you to take a look at the things that make you come alive, those natural talents that make you who you are, and once you get a list of those ten things that make you shine, ask yourself, "How can I go out and share those gifts in every aspect of my life?"

I will share with you a list I made, which I keep by my desk to remind me what I have to contribute to others:

1. My generosity

2. My willingness to help others/do charitable work

3. My ability to listen to people and have them experience feeling heard

4. My ability to see the best in people in any situation and to help them to see the best in themselves

5. My capacity to love others unconditionally

6. My ability to instantly relate with people and connect to them

7. My perseverance

8. My ambition/drive

9. My zeal for life

10. My fearlessness and ability to be unstoppable

As **homework**, make a list of ten of your own best attributes. Keep it where you work as an instant confidence boost when you need one, and as a way to remind yourself that in business, it pays much more to take pride in your positive qualities than it does to be too modest. This will also make a great starting place when you need to find something to highlight in your communications with potential employers.

## GETTING MORE THAN YOU GIVE

Whoever said that it is better to give than to receive was definitely correct. Whether you believe in karma, dharma or just doing something good for the sake of doing it, giving is one of the most powerful tools of successful people. Oprah Winfrey and Bill Gates present two perfect examples of this. Even though they both are worth billions they never stop figuring out ways to give back to those in need. Whether your idea of giving is to open a school in an impoverished area, feed the hungry, volunteer for your favorite charity or simply give your money to a charitable cause that you believe in, giving back can be an amazing source of fulfillment both personally and professionally.

Many of the most successful people use the wealth they have acquired to do something positive to contribute and give back to their communities. The more you make, the higher your status becomes, and the more people begin to look at you as a role model or example. There is nothing more powerful in this world than being able to be a positive influence for another human being.

Contribution comes in many forms. You can contribute money to a group or individual or make a difference by donating your time. Regardless of the form, there are thousands of organizations that need your assistance.

You do not have to be a celebrity or a billionaire to make a difference, though. Just look at Mother Teresa. She is a perfect example of one person who made a huge impact. Any one person can make a difference simply by acknowledging the people in their lives that make a difference. I once was asked to participate in an exercise where each day we were to acknowledge at least one person in our life. It is amazing the difference you can make in another person's life simply by thanking them. In my case, I spent each day acknowledging various people in my life, from my parents to the security guard who let me in every day in my building to the parking garage attendant, Juan, who made sure my car was safe while I was at work.

It is humbling to recognize that the little things in life can make the greatest impact. Imagine what life would be like if you refused to take anything for granted. If you thanked every person you encountered for the difference they make in your life. What would life be like? What would the world be like if we all took the time to acknowledge the everyday people who make a difference?

I encourage each of you to go out in your life and acknowledge at least one person for the difference they make. Doing this will not only make a difference in the other person's life, but can also greatly contribute to your own.

## ARE YOU REFERABLE?

Are you someone that others like to be around? Do you have a pleasing personality? Are you perceived by others as being professional and positive? Are you the type of person who gives back and contributes to others? Are you adding value to other people's lives?

These are just a few questions you can begin to ask yourself to find out if you are someone others are likely to refer. Why is being someone who is referable important? People are not going to go out of their way to recommend you to a potential employer if you are not someone that they would want to do business with. The same goes for potential employers. When you go in for an initial interview, it is up to the person who is screening you to decide whether or not YOU will make THEM look good to their higher ups.

This does not mean that finding a job is a popularity contest. It simply means that the more memorable you are (in a good way!), and the more people find you to be someone they would want to spend time with or do business with, the more likely it is that you will be recommended by that person. Here is a perfect example of a person who is unlikely to have a high referability value:

> Job Seeker Candidate A: "Here is my business card. I need a job ASAP and want you to recommend me to everyone you know. Things really suck right now. I was fired from my old job because my boss was a jerk who had it out for me and it was totally unfair that I was let go. I never get what I want and I do not even know why I bother coming to these events."

I wish this example were made up, but unfortunately I have seen some variation of this example in a variety of networking situations. From an outsider perspective, it is easy to see why Candidate A is unlikely to be recommended by anyone, let alone considered for a job by a potential employer. Now look at another example of a job seeker in the exact same situation, but who holds an entirely different perspective:

Job Seeker Candidate B: "How are you? How is your job search coming? I am so glad to be here. It is wonderful to get out and be around people who are so upbeat and have such a great attitude about finding a new job. Is there anything I can do to be a resource for you in your job search? I would love it if we could connect on LinkedIn and stay in touch. Could I get your information? Perhaps we could even grab a coffee to discuss our respective job searches and to see how we can help one another find our next jobs. I really look forward to getting to know you better."

It is obvious to see that Candidate B would is much more likely to be recommended to a potential employer, and would have a much higher referability value overall. Sometimes job seekers do not even realize they are being negative, and they wind up sabotaging themselves and their job search unintentionally. If this is the case for you, it is never too late to start anew. The following three tips to will help you become more referable both in a networking situation and in an interview:

1. Be positive. What is done is done. The past should not hold you back from what is possible in the future. Focus on what you are now creating.

2. Make it about other people. Always offer to be a resource for another person. The same goes with potential employers. Do not ask "Do you have a job for me?" Instead offer resources and solutions that will help the employer or other job seeker with their problem or need.

3. Be memorable. Spend some time crafting a strong "Tell me about yourself" statement. This will help you to stand out from the other job seekers who are fighting for a similar job to the one that you want.

If you want to see how referable you are, you might want to check out www.naymz.com or www.klout.com. These interesting social networking websites take referability to a whole new level wherein you are given a reputation score based on what people think of you in your network. It can be a valuable tool to see what your referability value is. If you discover that you are not as referable as you had hoped, do not be discouraged. You can always increase your referability value; just remember to be positive, be a resource and be memorable!

## ARE YOU GIVING UP TOO EASILY?

Have you ever found yourself wondering that if you had pushed yourself just a little bit harder you would have succeeded? I found myself thinking about this very question just the other night. I was playing a game on my iPhone at the airport called "Unblock Me." (Very appropriate name for this discussion!) It is a simple game that requires you to move blocks in different directions until your main colored block has a clear path to exit the puzzle.

I think this game can be a great analogy for life. You see, I had played this puzzle several times to no avail. It was not until about the fifth time that I realized that I was missing a critical move and was quitting the game too early. If I had just made that one additional move the whole puzzle would have unfolded very easily. This gave me an "ah-ha!" moment when I began to realize how many times in life I have stopped just short of my goal because I think the obstacles in front of me are too insurmountable, or that I have no moves left.

This analogy became even clearer to me when I attended a VIP networking event in San Francisco. When I first arrived at the party only a few people were there and I began talking to someone standing near me about business, with no intention of speaking to this person for more than a few minutes to pass the time.

There were a few key VIPs that I really wanted to speak with that night, so as the party began to fill up, I had already planned my exit strategy from that initial conversation. As luck would have it, I talked to this initial person longer than I had originally anticipated, and wound up getting some extremely valuable information about book publishing out of the conversation. I would have never gained that information if it were not for the fact that I had stayed that extra five minutes to talk to him.

Ask yourself this: How often have you stopped short of your goals? How many times do you give up because you think it will not make a difference?

Think about this tonight before you go to bed and make a list of the top ten things you wish you had accomplished, but stopped short of because of some obstacle. Then look at your list, pick one thing that you had given up on and begin to look at that thing from a new perspective. Write down ten ways that you could push through and achieve that goal if you really wanted to. Try to think outside of the box and look at this goal in a new way. Do not tell yourself "I cannot do it"; instead, ask yourself "How can I do it?"

If you can break through even one block, that can help to give you a clear path towards achieving your goals! When you break through just one of your blocks you are on your way to having everything you want out of life.

## IS AGEISM AN ISSUE?

Most of us are aware that even though it is illegal, ageism does exist. A number of companies will and do discriminate against people because of their age, among other things. However, ageism is not quite as prevalent as you might think. After having been a recruiter for over ten years, I can say that ageism does occur on occasion, but there are ways to mitigate its effects.

The first thing to note about ageism is that if a company is set on discriminating against you, it will. It is better not to waste energy fighting the battles you know you cannot win. You cannot change who you are, so focus on making the other aspects of your presentation as excellent as possible!

**Strategy #1:** Do not worry about posting a photo on social networking sites as long as it is a professional photo. I have had a lot of job seekers ask me if they should post their photo on websites such as LinkedIn, and my answer is always *yes*. A company is just as likely to discriminate against you based on a photo (even though it is illegal) as they will in person. Personally, I would not want to work for any company that would discriminate against me to begin with, so I would rather have them not call me in for an interview in the first place and waste my time. That is up to you. If you are concerned that your photo will knock you out of the running because you are "too old" that is at your discretion.

However, it is worse to use an outdated photo than a current one that "makes you look old." Showing up looking radically different than your online photo can seem suspicious—as can not having a photo at all.

**Strategy #2:** Only go back ten years on your resume, and do not bother listing your graduation dates. This is completely unrelated to protecting your age, Going back only ten years is just proper protocol agreed upon by most resume writers, recruiters and career coaches.

*Something to note:* If you worked at a particular company for thirty years, I would suggest listing all thirty years of your experience with that company. Some people may disagree with me, but my thoughts are that having strong stability on your resume is still a good thing. I have had others suggest that it can hurt you to list 1980–2010, but I have found that good companies still appreciate someone who is loyal and shows strong stability. There are certain companies that might discriminate based on this fact, but again, I would recommend avoiding these companies in the first place.

It is unnecessary for you to list when you graduated college, and thus you should not feel obligated to add your graduation dates unless you choose to. Putting a graduation date on a resume is a little more tricky than listing thirty years of experience or including a photo. If you put that you graduated in 1972, most people will automatically assume that means you are approximately 60 years old give or take a few years based on the average age people graduate college. The same calculation might not necessarily be made based on a simple photo or work history. My recommendation is not to list graduation dates as they are not as relevant to your overall resume.

**Strategy #3:** If you get to the interview stage, *don't make your age an issue*! If age is not already an issue for the company you are interviewing with, do not make it one! I once had a job seeker I was working with who was about to turn 60. I had never once considered her age, and sent her out to my clients the way I would any other candidate because she was just as qualified as anyone else. Unfortunately, she did not feel the same way. After her initial interview with a company I sent her to, I received a call back from a recruiting manager who said they were passing on her. The recruiting manager went on to explain that the job seeker had expressed concern several times during the interview about how old she was and whether the executives would like her. This recruiting manager thought she was well qualified for the position; however, after hearing the candidate's insecurities about her age, the recruiting manager was reticent to pass her resume along in the interview process. After getting this feedback I called the job seeker to softly coach her on the subject, and the next interview she went in for, she got the job!

Just remember, ageism is out there, but there are only a small percentage of companies that will discriminate based on your age. If you do not make your age an issue, most companies will not either! Look at your age as an asset, and so will the company you interview with.

## THE ADAPTABILITY FACTOR

There is an interesting chasm that we are noticing in the market right now. It is something that almost every law firm and corporation we work with has noticed as well. That chasm exists between the millennials and the baby boomers. The millennials have amazing technical skills and can complete a project, but often lack the work ethic, ability to be proactive and advanced skills that more seasoned workers possess. We often hear complaints from our clients about how the millennials are unable to take initiative and have a sense of entitlement regarding the work they do. On the flip side, the experienced workers/ baby boomers have tremendous skills and an amazing work ethic, but are unable to adapt to the changes in the marketplace. It is this fact, the "Adaptability Factor," that is inhibiting a lot of the more seasoned applicants from being able to get hired and then stay employed once they are hired.

What do I mean by this? I mean that one's ability to adapt in this marketplace directly correlates to how effective or ineffective one is at getting hired and staying employed in this market. I hear a lot of job seekers over the age of 50 who scream "Ageism!" as to why they are not being hired in this market; however, I have found that adaptability has a lot more to do with hire-ability than age does.

A perfect example of this is that my staffing firm has personally placed numerous people who are over the age of 50, 60 and sometimes even 70, but many of these more experienced workers who do get hired are subsequently fired because they are unable to adapt to the new skills that are required of them due to the changing expectations of employers.

There recently was an article in the *Wall Street Journal* about how legal secretary jobs are becoming obsolete. I disagree. I believe that legal secretary jobs are just as prevalent now as ever, although the role of the legal secretary has shifted tremendously. Years ago it was common to have one secretary to one attorney, where the secretary was interfacing with clients and acting as more of a personal assistant, in addition to filing documents.

In today's market, it is not unheard of for a legal secretary to support five, six or even seven attorneys. This is because the more junior associates are extremely self-sufficient and the attorneys who are using legal secretaries rely on them more for technical skills and knowledge. Legal secretaries are now doing word processing and paralegal work, as well as administrative work. Therefore, if you as a legal secretary cannot adapt to these new demands and expectations, your position will be eliminated. Employers everywhere are looking to cut costs and create more "hybrid" type roles where several positions are combined into one.

So how do you become more adaptable in this market if you are a more experienced worker who wants to get hired?

You shift your perspective. It will not do you any good to go around complaining about how old you are and how unfair it is that there are no jobs out there and how hard things have become. Instead, look at how fortunate you are to have twenty plus years in a changing marketplace and how if you can use your experience to your advantage by being willing to adapt to the new climate and marketplace, you WILL be the most desirable applicant. The next time you are in a temporary role or an interview, instead of explaining why you CANNOT do something, discuss what you CAN do and how willing you are to adapt to whatever is required of you. I truly believe that legal secretaries and other working professionals with many years of experience still have an important place in the current market if only they are willing to adapt and figure out HOW to make it work, rather than lament all the reasons it will not work.

# 6 | The Interview

*"Our deepest fear is not that we are inadequate. Our deepest fear is that we are powerful beyond measure. It is our light, not our darkness, that most frightens us. We ask ourselves, who am I to be brilliant, gorgeous, talented and fabulous? Actually, who are you not be?"*
*Marianne Williamson*

## THE INTERVIEW STARTS EARLIER THAN YOU THINK

Many job seekers are unaware that their interview starts long before they walk in the door. In fact, the moment someone calls you to set up a time for you to come in, the interview has begun. When the phone rings, and the human resources person introduces him- or herself, you should literally stand up, remember your preparation and communicate clearly your interest in the potential employer.

When you arrive at the parking lot and/or garage of the potential employer, it is critical to treat everyone, even the parking attendant, with the utmost respect. People can often be rude to each other in a parking garage by honking or by interacting on their cell phones. However, you never know if the person you are interviewing with might be the one you are honking at!

The same goes if you are riding up in the elevator to your interview. There could very well be a human resources manager or other key executive in the elevator with you and if you are not polite, or if you are chewing gum, it is bound to reflect negatively on you in the interview. One of the most common errors you can make is to be rude to the receptionist.

In the ten plus years I have spent as a recruiter, several of my clients would prescreen a candidate based on how well or poorly they treated the receptionist. Many people lost job offers over the years because of something as simple as being on a cell phone while waiting in the reception area or being rude.

Next time you have an interview, remember—it begins the moment you are invited in for the interview and continues every time you make contact with the business!

## MY BIGGEST PET PEEVE—MAKE TIME FOR YOUR INTERVIEWS!

When you are beginning to consider going out on interviews and you are currently working, it is critical that you set aside time for these interviews. One of the most frustrating things for a recruiter is to push a candidate in for an interview and have the candidate come back and say he or she cannot make it. When you are looking for a job you need to make yourself available during regular business hours Monday through

Friday between 8 a.m. and 6 p.m. On very rare occasions, an employer might be flexible and see you early in the morning or after work; however, most companies need you to interview during work hours.

If you ask a recruiter to submit you for a position and that person is able to get you an interview, it is very important to make the time to go. Most companies will give you options of several different days and times for interviewing. If you do not go on the interview that a recruiter or company has set up for you then it can reflect poorly on you as a job seeker and that company may not be willing to consider you again.

If you cannot set aside some time for interviews, then you are probably not ready to start your job hunt. One woman I coached told me that she was desperate for a job, but when I took her at her word and got her an interview for the very next day, she said she could not possibly go because she had not had her hair done! Whatever your hair looks like, you have a much better chance with the hairdo than if you just do not show up. Always be ready for an opportunity to interview!

The less flexible you are in the interview process and/or while you are temping, the less likely you are to be hired. Flexibility can be anything from being flexible with the times you are available to interview to being flexible with your attitude about the types of duties you are willing to do. If you are someone who is very accommodating and flexible throughout the process, the employer will take note and be more inclined to hire you.

I coached a man recently who was desperate for work—but turned down an eight-week assignment because it was not long enough for him and he was worried that it would negatively impact his unemployment. That assignment could have led to valuable experience and a long-term position or even possible full-time employment, but those opportunities were lost because the job seeker was not flexible enough to take a slight risk by utilizing a temporary job. It is good to know what you want, but even better to be able to see an unexpected opportunity and take advantage of it!

## RESEARCH

I had a candidate once who once obtained the position of assistant vice president at a bank. She had no college degree and five years' experience over two competitors who each had over fifteen years' experience and degrees. How? When asked why she wanted to work for the company, she produced a copy of its 10-K (earnings) report that she had researched on the Internet, highlighted with notes on what she was impressed by and suggestions for improving those results. This was part of what the job would entail, and her analysis blew their minds. The other two people she was up against never had a chance.

In another example, the most recent time that I went out of my way to try to place a job seeker from out of town (which is normally very difficult here due to the laws in California), it was because she approached me saying that she had read my website and knew my work. She discussed things that I had written about and said she specifically wanted to work with me. I ended up going out on the limb for her. I called some of my best contacts and would have had three interviews for her on the same day—if she had not accepted a job after the second one I set up for her! I was impressed by her research, and I am sure you would have been too. The same tactic works just as well with interviewers and important networking contacts.

One of the biggest keys is coming in to an interview knowing about the company. Use the Internet and social networks as well as word of mouth. How can you target your self-presentation and make yourself look specifically useful to the company if you do not know anything about the company?

## PRESENTATION

*"If you are on time, you are late. If you are early, you are on time."*

Your goal at the interview is to present yourself as well as possible, and this extends to a lot of areas. Always show up at least fifteen minutes early for your interview. For one thing, there is almost never any excuse for being late to an interview, and giving yourself a fifteen- to thirty-minute buffer will help prevent that from happening. Also, you can never say for sure how long other candidates' interviews will last, and if you have already arrived and announced yourself to the receptionist they may get to you early—allowing you to show yourself to be that much more on the ball.

While it is difficult to surmount the disadvantage of lateness, if something unavoidable does cause you to be late, it is essential to keep in good communication with the office you are trying to get to. If your car or your arm has just broken, it is always better to try to call and re-schedule than it is simply to assume that you have lost the opportunity. As with any important appointment, control the things you *can* control by arriving on time, and deal with the unavoidable if it happens.

> Karen was proud of herself for arriving to her interview over an hour early. She did not want to park in the company's parking lot that early, though, and instead opted to park next door at a nearby hotel so that she could take some time to review her notes on the company and the position. Upon leaving the parking lot, she got a flat tire. Rather than can-celling her interview she enrolled the help of the valet at the hotel to watch her car for her while she went for her inter-view. Most people would have given up, but her persever-ance paid off when she got rave reviews after her interview.

Your presentation once you get to the interview itself extends beyond your physical appearance. An impeccably prepared candidate can still look slovenly or agitated at the interview if she or he is pro-jecting the wrong kind of body language. This is another of those things that might seem obvious, but it is all too easy to forget. Uncross your arms and legs, sit up straight and relax your shoulders. The idea is to convey that you are attentive but not guarded, and what you do when sitting at your own desk or while socializing with your friends will probably not cut it when you are attempting to impress an inter-viewer. Keep in mind that your body language is just as important as what you are saying.

Look your interviewer in the eye when appropriate. You want to get across that you are listening to what is being said, and that you are being direct rather than evasive with your answers. Shake hands firmly and confidently. An interviewer's subconscious impressions of you from small indications such as this can be just as important as his or her con-scious impressions.

A lot comes down simply to paying attention to everything you do, and how that could affect your potential new bosses' opinions of you. Filling in your paperwork incompletely or with bad, unreadable penmanship can sometimes make you appear just as sloppy as if you *had* been late for an interview that you made it to on time.

In an interview, an employer comes up with an assessment about you within the first ten seconds of meeting you. This assessment then shapes how that employer interviews you. If the employer assesses you to be someone who is professional and trustworthy, then they are going to ask you questions and listen to you through the lens of someone who is trustworthy and professional.

If the employer assesses you to be someone who is unreliable and lacking composure, then the employer's questions and how they listen to you will be colored by that judgment. So how do you make the first ten seconds you have with an employer count?

1. Smile and project a positive attitude (leave your problems/concerns at home). An authentic smile is the universal signal that puts people at ease and makes them comfortable with you. In addition, a positive attitude makes others want to be around you and get to know you better.

2. A firm, but friendly handshake. Stay away from the dead-fish handshake or even worse, the bone-cruncher handshake. Instead, go with a firm but warm handshake while looking the person in the eyes.

3. Use open body language. Do not cross your arms or your legs, as this puts a barrier between you and the person you are meeting with. Be careful not to fidget.

4. Use a clean, sharp haircut or style with natural-looking makeup if you are a woman. It is important that your hair is gelled, blow-dried or pulled back. Frizzy, un-styled or unwashed hair can leave a bad first impression by making you appear unkempt.

## BODY LANGUAGE MISTAKES

Maintaining proper body language can be tricky since it consists of adjusting the involuntary things we do with our bodies without thinking, and it requires a spatial awareness that we may not be used to developing. Here are some of the most common body language gaffes to watch out for in your interviewing:

1. Tilting your head to the right or left. Doing this can make the interviewer think that you are not taking what they are saying seriously and can come off as flirtatious.

2. Leaning away from the interviewer and/or leaning back. This can make you seem disinterested in the conversation.

3. Crossing your arms or your legs. Crossing any part of your body during an interview puts a barrier between you and the person you are interviewing with.

4. Playing with or tossing your hair during the interview. This can come across as flirtatious or distracted behavior.

5. Overly gesticulating during the interview. It is appropriate to occasionally use your hands to illustrate a point during the interview, but too much hand movement can be a distraction to the person interviewing you.

## BE MEMORABLE

I personally interview anywhere from 5 to 20 people a week. Some weeks I remember almost everyone and other weeks I can barely recall whom I have met. The same is true of employers. They see hundreds of job seeker resumes for every open position, and then interview anywhere from 5 to 20 people per position on average. If you are up against anywhere from 5 to 20 other people in any average interview situation then you better bring your A-game. So how do you make yourself memorable?

1. Get a career coach or a friend to help you practice your answers to interview questions. I cannot begin to tell you how many times my eyes have glossed over during an interview when I hear the same uninspired answers to every interview question. Your friends are your friends for a reason, and they want to see you succeed as much as you do! Do not be shy about asking them to help with a practice interview.

2. Dress to impress. Dress sharp, but do not overdo it with loud colors or accessories. A job seeker I recently placed came in to interview with me one day and he blew my socks off. He had on a very sharp

suit and tie, nothing over the top, but I was immediately struck by how professional he came across. Needless to say, my client was equally as impressed and hired him on the spot.

3. Finally, it is important to remember that attitude is everything! You can be extremely well dressed and very articulate; however, if your attitude does not match everything else, you will quickly fade into the background. It is important to be confident, but not cocky. You should also be extremely eager to get the position, but not desperate. It is a very fine line, but when properly balanced, you will always be the one who stands out!

## WHAT NOT TO WEAR

You will notice I stress the importance of dressing to impress. Everyone thinks they know how to dress well, but people are still passed up at interviews every day because of their sartorial choices.

Many job seekers still do not know what is appropriate and what is not appropriate to wear in an interview. Often something as simple as what you wear can get you passed on for a position.

Here is my list of the top fifteen things not to wear in an interview:

1. Denim! It is never appropriate to wear denim to an interview.
2. A short skirt.
3. A t-shirt.
4. A dress or blouse that shows any sort of cleavage.
5. Dangling jewelry (this can distract the interviewer).
6. A backpack or big bulky bag.
7. Headphones, sunglasses or a cell phone earpiece.
8. Facial or body piercings or visible tattoos, including earrings on men (small earrings are OK for women) or heavy makeup.
9. Brightly colored or overly patterned clothing (this includes Hawaiian shirts).
10. Long acrylic nails.

11. Overly baggy or ill-fitting clothes (it makes you look frumpy).

12. Stained or wrinkled clothes.

13. Scuffed shoes, heels that are too high, or flip-flops.

14. No socks with your shoes—you must wear socks if you are a man, and they *must* match.

15. A heavy fragrance or perfume—this can lose you the position.

I recently had a job seeker ask if it was appropriate for her to wear a dress to the interview rather than a suit, since it was to take place on a Friday. I told her that adding a blazer to the conservative dress she was wearing would be perfectly acceptable. This did not turn out so well when the interviewer called me, distraught, to say that he was passing— and to ask why on Earth she had seen fit to show up in a denim mini skirt!

Look at what you are wearing and imagine you are the interviewer— how impressed would you be?

> Diane has an interview and has prepared well, but as soon as she arrives, her interviewer seems to receive her without interest and enthusiasm; she does not get the call for the job. Her interviewer was put off by the fact that Diane is missing her two front teeth—as are all the other interviewers who see her. Her qualifications are ignored and she soon becomes well-known in her industry by the nickname "Toothless"—and virtually unhirable.

We often like to think of appearances as skin deep, but when it comes to landing a job, things are not as simple as that. You and I know (and so does your potential employer) that there are a lot of things we simply cannot change. You cannot make yourself taller or shorter for a job, so it is no use fretting about your height—but if there is something very obvious about your appearance that you could correct and have not, an interviewer may start to wonder why.

It is not always an insurmountable obstacle (the only candidate I know of who's received an on-the-spot offer right at the interview did it by demonstrating hugely impressive subject knowledge—despite having several black teeth), but absolutely any edge you can give yourself is important.

> Style-conscious Tony chose his clothes very carefully when preparing for his big interview. He dressed neatly and expensively, but when the interview took place he was not considered for the position after the interviewer was shocked to see that Tony was not wearing any socks. When he was given feedback on his faux pas later, Tony defended his decision on that basis that "those are Gucci shoes! You do not wear socks with Gucci shoes, darling!"

When your interviewer is not likely to be familiar with the designer of your shoes, you do wear socks. Or wear another pair of shoes. But no matter what, it is important to get a sense of the commonly accepted notion of businesslike respectability, and follow it. It is almost always true that while employers look for candidates with originality, they do not want that originality to make itself immediately visible in their wardrobe or physical appearance.

Unless you have a good sense already of what your prospective employer's dress code and workplace environment are like, it is safer to err on the conservative side. This can be difficult for many people, as having to subdue a style of dress or self-presentation can feel like subduing personal identity. But to avoid the risk of repelling a potential hirer by going past their limits on what constitutes respectability you should dress conservatively.

> Laura had been working with me for some time on developing a killer resume, networking and interview skills. She was thrilled to get an interview with one of the top law firms in the country, and brought her A-game to the interview process. She aced the first four interviews, and for the fifth level of interview she wanted to do something to give her an edge and push her to the next level of getting the job. Unfortunately, the scented lotion she decided on was so strong that the plan backfired—Laura was rejected based just on that.

You want your interviewer to think more about you than about what you look or smell like. Anything too distracting or overpowering is too much. It is better to smell like nothing at all or to dress so inconspicuously that your clothes are forgotten as soon as you leave as long as *you* leave a good, memorable impression.

## TALKING POINTS

When politicians appear on television and radio they rarely fail to seem self-assured and to get across just the message that they want to, regardless of the question that they have been asked. In short, they do just what you want to do at your job interview. Remember to focus not on telling your interviewer exactly what they want to know, but on exactly what you want them to know. The way politicians do this—and the way you can too—is with a simple list of talking points that are broad enough that they can be returned to time and again no matter the specifics of the question being asked.

For **homework**, come up with a list of ten talking points to bring into interviews. These will change somewhat depending on the interviews, but they should always contain a concise list of your most attractive attributes to a potential employer, and you should always know a "roadmap" to get back to your talking points no matter what you are asked. It will not only optimize your answers, but help you to respond confidently every time and never be stuck for an answer when you know that you have relatable material ready at hand.

Your goal is to appear confident (without appearing arrogant), and the surest way to do this is actually to be as confident and prepared as possible. Do not be intimidated by what could be awkward silences; fill these and use them to drive home your strongest talking points. Here is a **homework** exercise to help build your confidence: Come up with a list of ten things you have done that stand out in your current or most recent job. For each of those ten things give a concrete example that shows your effectiveness (see "The Evidence" section later in this part) in that area. You will feel more confident when you finish writing the list or when you review it—and when you have finished the list it will be great material to use to illustrate your talking points in the interview itself!

Look at this list, and go back to your original list of ten of your positive attributes from earlier. Together they are a treasure trove of great material to draw from as you are putting together which "talking points" to drive home in your contact with companies.

## BLOCK AND BRIDGE

Do you know the trick that every politician and TV personality uses in their interview? It is the simple task of blocking and bridging. The next time you watch a politician being interviewed about their campaign or a movie star about their next big blockbuster, watch the way they block and bridge to make a point.

Blocking and bridging simply means addressing the question that was asked, such as "Why is the sky blue?" and then blocking that question and bridging over to an answer that relates to a point you want to get across. Example: A politician is asked "Why is the sky blue?" but actually wants to discuss health care reform. He would then answer something like "I was just admiring the blue sky today on my drive to this speech. As I was admiring the blue sky, I began considering the implications of the current state of health care in this country and realized that I had to do something about it . . ." This is a very simple example, but you can see where I am going with it.

Politicians and celebrities do this because they have an agenda or a point they want to convey and often are not asked direct questions that allow them to relay this point.

You, as a job seeker, can use this same tactic during an interview. When asked ANY question in an interview, your goal should always be to look at where you can emphasize a point about why they should want to hire you. You should always have a list of ten or more talking points that you want to cover during your interview. You should be able to hit all ten of your interview talking points depending on how you block and bridge.

I want to be clear. I am not saying not to answer the questions you are being asked. I am suggesting that you answer the questions you are asked intentionally to get a point across that you are the right candidate for the job, that is, you should make the strongest case for why they should hire you instead of your peers.

I once spoke with an interviewer for a big company who passed on a great piece of advice for job seekers. She said, "Through your entire interview, pretend I have a big sign on my forehead that says, 'What can you do for me?'"

If you can turn that into a talking point, and then block and bridge your way to it, then you are on just the right track.

## PROACTIVE VS. REACTIVE INTERVIEWING

What is the difference between a proactive vs. a reactive interview?

A majority of the job seekers in today's market are passive interviewees who wait for questions to be asked of them (reactive). The difficulty with this style of interviewing is that you are waiting to be asked the "right" questions so that you can give the "right" answers. This style of interviewing is not bad or wrong, but it does make it more challenging to make your case on why you should be hired. When you are interviewing from the "reactive" approach, you have little to no control over how the interview will go. It is also much more boring and tedious for the person interviewing you when they have to pull information out of you one question at a time.

A proactive interview, on the other hand, is one where the job seeker has talking points prepared about what makes them suitable for the position and finds ways to incorporate these points into the interview (see the previous "Block and Bridge" section). A proactive candidate will also anticipate any possible concerns that the employer may have about their background such as lack of skills, movement on their resume, etc., and will proactively address these concerns throughout the interview before the interviewer brings them up. The great thing about this style of interviewing is that the candidate will not have to be on the defensive when a touchy point is brought up because it has already been handled proactively. When you proactively interview, it makes the interviewer's life easier because the interview flows more comfortably, and it makes your life easier because you can more readily address the points you want in order to make the strongest case for why they should want to hire you.

Example:

Candidate A has a good resume but recent movement on their resume.

The employer asks Candidate A: "Tell me about yourself."

Reactive interviewee:

"I have been in my field over ten years and am good at what I do."

Proactive interviewee:

"I have been in my field over ten years and love what I do. One thing that makes me stand out from others in my field is XYZ (talking point #1). Additionally, I want to point out that I do realize that I have moved around quite a bit recently and want to go through my history with you so that you can have a better picture as to why I have made some of these moves." Candidate A then proceeds to clearly paint a picture that depicts their reasons for leaving (RFL), anticipating the employer's potential concern about their movement (proactively addressing a potential concern AND saving the employer from painstakingly having to go through each RFL one by one).

As my example illustrates, proactive interviewing skills can easily enhance your effectiveness in your next interview and get you one step closer to the job offer you want.

Reactive interviewing can put you on the defensive and have you miss key opportunities to strengthen your case for why the employer should hire you.

As discussed, one reason that people are ineffective at interviewing is that they are unprepared for the concerns, hesitations and/or issues that an employer has about their background. Rather than proactively addressing potential concerns or issues regarding their own resume they wait to react to the questions the employer asks them about why they might NOT be a fit and typically fumble.

Following are some examples of potential issues or concerns an employer might express about your resume and/or background:

Why do you have so much movement on your resume?

Why do you not have a degree? or Why are you missing XYZ certification?

Why have you been temping so long?

What have you been doing since you were laid off?

Why do you not have specific experience or skills for this position?

The next time you go in for an interview, take a moment to dissect your resume the way an employer would, that is, look for reasons why someone would NOT hire you. From there, you can prepare talking points to address those potential issues/concerns during the interview (because chances are that those concerns will come up). When you proactively address those concerns about your resume, the employer will appreciate it AND you will enhance your effectiveness in relaying what makes you a good fit for the position.

## PEP

A good way to come up with a set of simple and memorable attributes to hammer home to your interviewer is with the mnemonic PEP, which stands for productivity, efficiency and performance. These three areas are of prime importance to any company, and the more you can convince your interviewer that you will increase PEP, the better your chances. Just about any question you are asked can and should be answered in a way that comes back to how you can increase these values at the company, or how you have done so elsewhere.

Over the years I have had the chance to get to know hundreds of C-level executives and hiring managers, and the question on all of their minds when you go in for an interview is: "How are YOU going to make my life easier?"

Regardless of whether they are the executive you will be directly reporting to or the human resources manager responsible for hiring you, they all have one thing in common: they want to look good. Everyone has someone they are responsible for reporting to; even a CEO has to report to investors and/or board members. In an interview, it is YOUR JOB to convey to the person that you are interviewing with how you are going to make their life easier and make them look good to their superiors. Hammering home your PEP is a concise and memorable way to do this. In order for you to effectively share your PEP with the interviewer, you must be able to clearly communicate what you are going to do for them and how doing that will alleviate some of their stress, while making them look great at the same time.

To find your personal PEP, look at your past work experience, and pinpoint examples of where you have increased the overall productivity, efficiency and/or performance of the organization that you worked for. These examples of your PEP can then be incorporated into your talking points. It is important to be able to explain the problem that you solve and the group of people that you solve it for in relation to the position you are applying for. You should be able to concisely explain what actions you have taken in the past that have had you be effective, and how that effectiveness, in turn, led to a smoother and less stressful working environment.

Do not just tell the executive WHAT you did, but also tell him or her how that impacted the company's performance and how you will be able to apply your PEP in your next position. Find out what problem it is that the executive needs to solve, and then formulate a solution and explain how that plan will be executed effectively. By doing this, you will be able to make a strong case for why YOU should be the next person hired.

Keep in mind that the interview is all about what you can do for the company. By staying "on message" the way a politician would, you are actually directing the conversation along the most relevant possible lines. When an interviewer asks you whether you work better in groups or individually, it is much less helpful to say simply, "I work better with others," than it is to stick with your PEP talking points and explain that, "I work better with others because I can always get more done more quickly when there are a lot of ideas in the mix and people help to solve each other's problems; the quality of the work is always greater if we can get more people's creative input involved to prevent or solve any issues."

## "TELL ME ABOUT YOURSELF"—WHY YOU NEED AN ELEVATOR SPEECH

You have probably heard it before, and you will probably hear it again. The most common, the most open-ended and perhaps the most important question asked in interviews or in networking situations is not technically a question but "Tell me about yourself."

Because there is no immediately obvious "right" or "wrong" answer to this prompt, it tends to make a lot of people freeze up in a very un-impressive way—but it need not do that to you. Like all questions you will be asked, this is an opportunity to present yourself in a positive light and emphasize the key points that you want the interviewer to take away.

However, there is one important thing not to do—do not tell your life story or start reading from your resume! Your "tell me about your-self" statement should *not* be your biography!

A good way to approach this goal when confronted with "The Question" is what I call an "Elevator Speech." Essentially, an Elevator Speech is a 30- to 60-second sound bite that highlights what you do, as well as what makes you stand out from others in your position—short but punchy enough that you can give it during an elevator ride and still be remembered. If an Elevator Speech is done well, it will not only make you memorable, but will also spotlight your uniqueness in an ef-fective way. One of the best introductions to an Elevator Speech I have ever heard was from an IRS man who, when asked what he did, simply replied "I am a government fundraiser."

Using humor is a risk that can pay off enormously, or can fall flat on its face. In an interview situation, it is usually better to be conservative and hold off on the jokes until you have a better idea of the person you're deal-ing with (even if you do know the interviewer, too many jokes can make you seem as if you don't take the opportunity or the situation seriously).

What is important here is not getting a laugh, but getting attention, backing it up and holding on to it. There are four main components to a great Elevator Speech:

1. Catch their attention.

2. Tell them what you offer or contribute.

3. Give an example that illustrates the benefit of what you offer.

4. Leave them wanting to learn more.

## THE HOOK

Your "Tell Me About Yourself" (or TMAY) statement could be one of the most important things you ever say. Giving a great one can open many doors for you and can help you land your dream job or business deal! So what makes one great? One of the most critical elements of your TMAY is your "hook." If you have a good hook the rest flows easily.

Your Elevator Speech should start with a tagline, which can be likened to the tagline that might be used to advertise a Hollywood movie: It encapsulates as briefly and wittily as possible the concept of the movie and why you should want to see it. How do you create a good hook?

It does not have to be hard work. There is a very simple and easy to use formula to quickly capture the attention of your audience. Here is what the formula looks like: "You know how a certain problem exists (X)? Well what I do is provide a unique solution to that problem (Y)." The idea is that you start off by describing a problem (X) faced by a group of people, and then you explain how you solve that problem in a unique, effective and memorable way (Y). The reason you want to do this is that most people start off by telling you *what* they do, instead of telling you how they can solve your problem. I learned this from an interesting class that I did on being effective at selling yourself and getting clients when you own a business (https://clientattractionsummit.com/). It is also relevant to job seekers because you are trying to get the potential employer to buy what you are selling, which is you! When you talk to people in terms of problem and solution, they become much more engaged and interested in what you have to say!

My hook to my own TMAY looks something like this: "You know how millions of Americans are struggling right now because they are out of work? Well, what I do is I coach job seekers prior to every interview to help them land their dream jobs."

It is simple and to the point, but at the same time powerful. I was saying my TMAY to someone at a coffee shop, and the person standing next to him overheard me and asked me for my business card. I later wound up coaching that person on his career all because he overheard my TMAY statement.

If you want to know if your TMAY is effective, practice it! The next time you go to a party or networking event and someone asks you what you do, say *only* your hook and shut up. If you have said your hook well and intrigued your audience, there will always be a follow-up question such as "How do you do that?" or "Tell me more about that." It is a great way to gauge how effective your hook is. If someone immediately loses interest after your hook, then you know you have to go back and rework it.

Remember, you want to entice your listener—*give them a taste of the milk but not the whole cow!*

## THE "WHAT" STATEMENT

Once you have your audience hooked, whether in an interviewing situation or a networking situation, the next step is to say a bit more about *what* you do, without having them lose interest. You want to cite specific results that you have produced in the past which correlate to what you are offering now.

In other words, if I were to begin discussing what a great artist I am, it would be immediately apparent that this has nothing to do with what I can offer you as a career coach or recruiter. Instead, I would specifically substantiate what I had just claimed and go into more depth as to the specific services my company offers such as one-on-one coaching and workshops. Where people falter is when it comes to discussing what they do in an interesting and informative way. Your hook starts by telling them about the problem that you solve and the group of people that you solve it for, and then your What Statement should expound upon your hook in more detail. Following is an example of my hook and my What Statement:

> "(*Hook:*) You know how millions of Americans are struggling because they are out of work and cannot find a job? Well what I do is I coach job seekers on how to land their perfect job in less than six months. (*What:*) How I do this is by determining the individual's strengths and weaknesses, helping them to create a personalized Wishlist, Statement of Intent and Daily Declaration."

Notice how I do not go into too much depth with my "What Statement." Your What Statement should be short, sweet and to the point. People often lose interest if you go too much into the technical aspect of what you do too quickly. Your What Statement should only be one to three sentences and should paint a broad picture of how you solve the problem you mentioned in your hook. Once you have done your hook and your WHAT statement, there is only one more step to perfecting your TMAY.

## THE EVIDENCE

The final aspect of your TMAY is your "evidence." Anyone can say that they can give the best massage or sell the best insurance package or offer the best legal advice, but unless you can back that statement up with strong evidence that supports your case, what you say is worthless.

Once you have elaborated on your tagline with the facts about yourself, you will want to elaborate by giving an example of where you were successful in one of those areas. For instance, in the situation I have been describing, I might say:

> "I recently gave a workshop where one of the participants was an animator who had been looking for a job for over a year. Less than two weeks after completing my workshop he landed his dream job teaching animation at a university, thanks to the information he learned in my workshop."

Using a strong, dramatic example of where you have been effective such as this one can have an enormous impact, but The Hook and the What part of your TMAY are meaningless if you cannot provide an example that supports what it is you are promising. For example, if I were to tell you that I am the world's best recruiter and that I can find you a job in less than six months, but I could not give you an example of where I have actually done this, then chances are I would not seem very impressive. You would assume I was making it up and move on—and a great Hook and What Statement would have been wasted.

Giving evidence as part of your TMAY is something that is often forgotten or overlooked. People will talk for hours about what they do or they will make big promises to you about what they can provide, but when it comes to giving an example or evidence to support what they are saying, people fall flat.

This is why having evidence is such an integral part of your TMAY. When you are considering what your hook is going to be, you should first think about an example that you have that backs up your hook statement.

Remember, the basic formula to an effective TMAY is as follows:

HOOK + WHAT + EVIDENCE =
A great TMAY that will get you the job!

You are not going to stand out or be memorable if you just state your name and what you do or, even worse, launch into your life story. People are interested in what you can provide for them, that is, what benefits you can offer to the organization you are interviewing with or the person you are networking with. Remembering your PEP mnemonic of productivity, efficiency and performance will serve you well here. Each element of your Elevator Speech should serve to illustrate how you bring PEP to a business. What you are really doing is marketing yourself; what you want to do is to tell the truth in a way that makes it sound as interesting as possible.

Finally, to quote P. T. Barnum, when you close any Elevator Speech you want to "always leave them wanting more." Make sure your audience is hungry and interested to keep learning about you and/or the services you provide.

I might close my speech with:

"Over my past ten years in career counseling and recruiting, I have had the pleasure of making a contribution to thousands of job seekers through coaching each individual on increasing their effectiveness and confidence. That has led to hundreds landing their dream jobs."

If you were in a networking situation you would want to follow up with what a great referral you would be. However, in an interview, you merely want to intrigue the interviewer such that they are eager to learn more about you and what you can offer.

As **homework**, *make a brief, gripping Elevator Speech for yourself*. Do this whether you think you already have your dream job or are looking for the first job you will ever have. I guarantee you will encounter situations where you will be glad you have this speech prepared.

## SUBJECTS TO AVOID

There are many subjects that you need to tread lightly around when in an interview. The following are the top four subjects that can quickly ruin your candidacy for a particular position.

1. Politics. This should go without saying, but I have noticed a lot of people bringing up politics in interviews whenever there has been a recent election. In addition, be careful about posting controversial or political topics on social media accounts like Facebook, Twitter and/or LinkedIn. Employers will Google you and see what you are saying. If they do not agree with you, they may not hire you. Even if there is not an election going on, you still want to be careful about what you share in an interview or on a social media site regarding your political affiliations.

   I heard of a situation in which a candidate went to an interview and did very well—until she started explaining her theory of how the government was secretly controlled by aliens. A personal belief like this is obviously outside of the norm but it should not hurt you in the workplace—unless you do not keep it to yourself in inappropriate contexts such as an interview.

2. Religion. Even though employers are not supposed to discriminate against you based on religious beliefs, you do not want to test that rule and bring up religious affiliations in an interview. Religion is a very hot topic that can easily offend the person you are interviewing with if their views are not in line with yours.

3. Sexual Preference. Sexual preference is another area that is protected under the Equal Opportunity Employment Commission (EEOC), but it is still a topic to be careful about discussing during an interview. Though many companies have become more forward thinking when it comes to this subject, you still don't

want to get into too much personal information during the interview process.

4. Personal Relationships. Discussing issues related to current or past personal relationships is typically not appropriate during the interview process. I often see people who discuss too much personal information in an interview, and this puts off many potential employers. Personal relationship information you may want to stay away from in an interview includes recent divorces, cheating, bad breakups, etc. This is none of the employer's business.

## DO YOU HAVE EXPERIENCE IN . . .

A job seeker recently asked me, "How do I handle it if I am asked about my experience in an area that I have not worked or am not experienced with?" This question can often come up in an interview. The interviewer might ask you: "How strong are your Excel (Excel could be anything) skills?"

If you did not have prior experience working with Excel, but were familiar with it, you might want to reply something like this: "I have always wanted to learn Excel. It is software that I am familiar with, but have not had the opportunity to use extensively in my past positions. It is something I am sure I could pick up quickly, especially given my knowledge of other Microsoft Office tools such as Word and Outlook." It also would not hurt to give an example of where you picked up something similar quickly.

In this case you do not want to specifically talk about the lack of your skills in that area. Instead, you want to emphasize where you do have skills and how those skills can be parlayed into whatever they want you to learn. Always de-emphasize what you don't know and emphasize what you do know.

## ATTITUDE

Remember—attitude is still everything. Now that a positive outlook has helped you to land the interview, you need to put that attitude to work for you in landing the position. If you go into an interview, and make it all about what the employer can offer you, they are not going to be interested. They want to know what is in it for them if they hire you.

The only time I have ever had a job seeker get a job offer right at the interview, it was a candidate who you might not even have expected to get in the door. She was overweight, disheveled and had decaying teeth, but because she was so on the ball and prepared, and brought the right attitude to the interview, she proved that your value to the company is more important than your physical attributes.

## DELIVERY MAKES THE DIFFERENCE

It is not what you say as much as how you say it. This is very true, especially in interviews. Following are some examples of what people say in an interview versus what they are trying to say.

Example 1:

*What was said:*

INTERVIEWER: "Why did you leave your last job?"

JOB SEEKER: "The company closed."

*What could have been said:*

JOB SEEKER: "I was at my last job over five years and loved everyone there, which is why I stayed as long as I did. Unfortunately, due to things slowing down, they had to restructure, but I am grateful for everything I learned there and look forward to applying it in my next position."

Example 2:

*What was said:*

INTERVIEWER: "Why should we want to hire you?"

JOB SEEKER: "I am hard working, detail oriented and organized."

*What could have been said:*

JOB SEEKER: "I have spent over ten years in the field and I love what I do. A few things that make me stand out are probably the facts that I am very detail oriented and organized. An example of where that proved useful in my most recent position was when we were working on a large project that didn't have any structure. I took the lead on the project and implemented a new organizational system that help cut the time of the project in half from the initial projections."

These two examples show how job seekers can increase their ability to sell themselves in an interview through better delivery and communication. Almost everyone I have ever interviewed has at least one example of where they have been effective, but often they are not clear on how to deliver that information in an interview.

## FIND A COMMON GROUND

This is key: People like to hire people who are like themselves. At a recent workshop I led on interviewing in downtown Los Angeles, a question came up that I had never encountered before, but it definitely got my wheels turning:

"What do I do if my conversational cadence does not match that of the person that I am interviewing with?"

This question surprised me because I have coached thousands of people over the years on many aspects of being effective in an interview, but this was one subject I had not thought to include in my workshops. After giving the question some thought, I realized that being able to match another person's conversational cadence is not something that comes naturally to a lot of people. I also realized what a critical component conversational cadence is an interview, and how it can make or break the interview.

Often, we take it for granted that we are able to have flowing conversations with the people closest to us, such as our friends and family. We do not realize how difficult it is to match someone else's pace until we are in an interview setting (or in some cases a date!) where it is blatantly clear that things are not meshing. So why is it so easy to converse with your friends and family and yet so nerve-racking to speak to someone new in an interview (or in any situation, for that matter)? The reason for this is that we naturally adjust our rhythm and style to fit that of those that we are closest to. Think about your closest friend. Chances are, you speak in a similar fashion when you are together. This happens over years of spending time together and adjusting to each other's styles.

How can you apply the same principles of how you interact with your friends to being successful in an interview?

The answer is simple: Mimic them. By mimicking the person you are interviewing with, you will put them at ease, and you might surprise yourself by how comfortable you feel. What makes friendship so easy is that over the years we unintentionally wind up mimicking each other's behaviors. People like people who are like themselves. The same is true of potential employers. Just like married couples who wind up looking alike or pet owners who wind up with pets that look strangely similar to their owners, people like to hire people like themselves.

I am not saying that you have to run out and dress up like the person you are interviewing with. Quite the contrary—I am simply asking you to become more aware of how you interact with other people and get more in tune with different people's respective styles. Styles can range from voice pitch, to what is said, to how it is said. A way to practice mimicking others is to find someone who is very "high energy," almost to the point that you find them annoying. Then try to match their energy level and conversational pace just like you would with a friend.

The same goes for someone who is very "laid back" or low energy. Try to bring your energy down to mirror that of the person who you are with. It is not quite as easy as it sounds, but it is better to practice with people you know then take your chances in an interview with a complete stranger.

Once you have become more adept at mimicking those around you, go out and try it in the real world. Try it out on dates, and in normal everyday situations. The more effective you become at mimicking other people's behavioral styles, the more successful you will find yourself in interviews. The key is to gauge another person's style and meet them at their level. If the person you are interviewing with loves to use big words such as "loquacious," then throw in your own multisyllabic words. The more present you become to how people interact the more success you will have in your own interactions, and most importantly, in your interviews!

## REALLY BEING THERE—THE ART OF INTENTIONAL LISTENING

So how do you become "present?" Being able to actively listen is one thing, but having the ability to discern what the other person really wants is an art form. In today's competitive market, it is more important than ever to have a leg up on the competition. One way to make yourself stand out in an interview situation is to intentionally listen for what the other person wants or needs.

Most people listen to others through a filter. In fact, study after study has shown that people listen effectively only 25% of the time! People often hear only what they want to hear, and do not pay close enough attention to what is said, and more importantly, to what is not said. Imagine the last time you were having a conversation and your mind began to wander to what you had for breakfast or to the list of errands you had to run. People do not typically listen to what others have to say; rather, they are simply waiting for their turn to offer their opinion or ideas. The same is true for interviewing.

When you are in an interview, you are often wrapped up in trying to think of the next question the interviewer might ask you or perhaps how to convince them to hire you. Rarely do people listen for what the employer needs and how they can solve the employer's problem. If you can learn how to listen for the problems a company needs solved and then turn around and offer a solution, you will blow the competition away!

Following are three tips to help you become a more intentional listener:

1. Be present. Empty your mind and focus on what the other person is saying, rather than your next response. Be willing to focus all your attention on what the other person is saying. It can be draining to be present all of the time, but in the long run, it is worth it.

2. Think/Listen empathetically. Be sensitive to the other person's feelings and thoughts. Avoid using the word "but," as it negates anything that was said prior. Focus on repeating back to the person what was said in a way that has the other person feel understood, such as "I can see why you would feel that way."

3. Ask questions and offer insights. Great listeners want to make sure they understand the problem clearly. They ask pertinent questions related to the conversation and will add ideas or insights to what the speaker has already said. This will give the speaker the experience of being heard.

Intentional listening takes hard work and focus. It can take an hour or a minute to hear what the other person is saying; that is up to you. If you take the time to work on your intentional listening skills, you will be amazed at what you hear.

## COMMON PITFALLS

Being in the recruiting world has been an interesting experience. I love career coaching, and now I get to bring career coaching to the job seekers that I am helping to find jobs. It has been interesting debriefing job seekers after interviews and then getting the feedback directly from the clients as to what was missing from the job seeker in a particular interview. Often it is simple things such as a lack of a certain skill set or not the right personality fit; however, more and more I am noticing some common mistakes that job seekers are making that could be easily avoided. The following are the top most common mistakes job seekers make in their interviews and how these mistakes can be remedied.

1. **Lack of knowledge in the position and/or company.** I recently had two job seekers go on interviews for completely different jobs, and both candidates were passed on immediately due to their lack of knowledge about the position. Knowing why you want to work for a company is one of the most important components of an interview. Especially in these challenging times, it is more important than ever to thoroughly research a company prior to an interview. In both cases, the candidates had barely skimmed the client's website. They had shown little to no knowledge when the client had asked them what particulars they knew about the company. This is one of my biggest pet peeves. It is frustrating as a recruiter to go out of your way to get a candidate an interview, to prepare the candidate and then to have the candidate not prepare themselves for the interview. This is a mistake that can be easily avoided. Just remember, as your **homework before the interview**, *always come up with at least five reasons why you want to work for a company, five reasons why they should want to hire you, and five questions regarding the position!*

Jim goes in for an interview with a major real estate company. When asked why he would like the accounting manager position for this particular company, he astounds the potential employer by his thorough research and knowledge of the company. He begins by addressing the fact that the president of the company loves racing (a subject that only the most thorough research would provide). He goes on to discuss the recent awards and accolades that the company has received and the real estate magazine article that the company was featured in. Due to his thorough due diligence and knowledge of the company, Jim received an offer later that same day.

2. **Cockiness.** This may seem like something I should not have to address, but it comes up as an issue. Being confident in yourself and your abilities is wonderful. Everyone should be able to list at least five reasons why a company should want to hire him or her, but using behavior or words that give evidence that you feel that you are entitled to the position is something entirely different. There is a fine line between cockiness and confidence. A way to avoid coming across as cocky in an interview is to avoid talking only about yourself, and to ask the employer questions about how you can help them and be a resource for them if you were to be hired. A cocky person would just go on and on about themselves, and would not be concerned about the company's needs.

3. **Bad "thank you" letters.** I have seen a variety of thank you letters over the years, and I am still amazed at what people will put into them. The most common mistakes are **bad grammar, misspellings, overzealous enthusiasm about the job** (I once had a candidate who had their job offer rescinded due to an overly enthusiastic email sent with exclamation points and happy faces. NO I am not joking!), and sometimes, **poor writing skills.** The easiest way to avoid these common pitfalls is to always ask someone else to proofread any thank you letter before it is sent out.

4. **Ineffective "Tell me about yourself" (TMAY) statements.**
Yours should be well thought out and well executed. From attorneys to file clerks, many job seekers have never been taught how to give a great TMAY statement. Make sure to have your Elevator Speech ready!

5. **Lack of enthusiasm/interest in the position.** The MOST important aspect of any interview, even more important than what you say, is your attitude. Who you are being in the interview has a lot to do with how successful or unsuccessful you may be. The people who do the best in any interview are not only the ones who are prepared, but also the ones who show the most enthusiasm and interest in the position. You could have prepared exceptionally well, but if your whole interview is done in a monotone voice, or just comes across as lackluster, chances are you are *not* going to be the one to get the job. The next time you go into an interview, try to think about something you are passionate about or excited about. I was recently interviewing a man who was not that excited during the interview. I proceeded to ask him what his favorite hobby was, and he started to share with me about surfing. His whole face lit up and he was a new person. I coached him to bring that same energy and enthusiasm to his next interview, and he did.

Watch out for these simple pitfalls in your next interview. If you prepare well, come across as confident, give a great "tell me about yourself," show enthusiasm and write a great thank you letter, you will be the one who likely gets the job!

## GOING THE EXTRA MILE (PROPER PREPARATION!)

Three to five years ago things were different. You did not have to *try* to get a job offer; in fact, you were probably solicited with more job offers then you knew what to do with. That said, things have changed. Although employers are beginning to hire again, it is a slow but steady process. For you, the job seeker, this means you have to go the extra mile!

What does going the extra mile mean to you? For some, it might mean simply ironing their shirt before the interview, or doing a little more research. But for others the extra mile is much longer! Following are a few ways to go above and beyond to make sure you *ace* your next interview.

- Know WHO you are meeting with. The normal job seeker will simply look up the person they are interviewing with on the company's website. The one who gets the job will go onto the company's website, Google, and LinkedIn and will thoroughly find out the preferences of the person they are meeting with. In some cases, they may even bring an appropriate gift based on the potential employer's interests (this is more appropriate for people in sales, marketing and higher level executive positions).

- Know WHAT you are interviewing for. Recruiters can be good and bad. Some recruiters will simply give a candidate they are working with the basic information about the job; however, it is YOUR job to go and dig deeper to find out WHAT the position is really about. If you want to go the extra mile in finding out WHAT the job is about, you can use resources such as LinkedIn and Twitter to see what people inside the company are saying about the position and/or research people on LinkedIn who have had the position before. You can also push your recruiter to see if there is any additional information about the job that will help facilitate your getting the offer.

- Know WHERE you are going for your interview. The average person will Google search the address of the place they are going for the interview to get directions. The person who goes the extra mile will DRIVE BY the location of their interview in advance to make sure they will not get lost on the day of the interview and eliminate as much as possible the disastrous possibility of lateness.

By knowing the WHO, the WHAT and the WHERE you will be one step closer to landing your next job!

Offer to do more! This is true for an interview or a temporary assignment. In an interview, prepare more than is expected and I guarantee you will blow the socks off of the next person you interview with. The same is true when you are working on a contract and/or temporary assignment. Just putting forth that extra little bit of effort can really get you noticed and have you stand out. There are many things that we know we could do to go above and beyond, but we get lazy or lackadaisical. It literally pays to be the person who expends the extra effort to achieve that payoff.

## WHAT TO AVOID

All the positive examples in the world cannot necessarily help warn you away from moves that could be big mistakes! Sometimes even "going the extra mile" can be a mile too far if it hits the wrong note; this is an area where you just have to exercise your social skills to make sure you have not gone too far. Sometimes the line can be very thin; I heard of a man who got a position after he sent a shoe to a company with a note explaining that it was his way of "getting his foot in the door." That might be a great way of going the extra mile, but you need to pull it off right. I recently heard from one company about how they summarily rejected a candidate who had randomly given them a pair of shoes for no apparent reason. Context is important!

Here are some of the biggest mistakes that I have seen candidates commit over the years:

- Leaving your cell phone on. This mistake is an absentminded oversight in many cases, but it can be a very dangerous one. A ringing cell phone sends the message that you do not care about the interview enough to shut out whoever may be calling or texting you—and that is not the kind of impression that gets you hired. One of the only things worse is to answer the cell phone!

- Chewing gum or sucking on candy during the interview. Not only is this highly distracting, but it is also quite disrespectful and can make it difficult for you to articulate at a time when you should be trying to make the best impression possible.

- Accepting a drink. This is not impolite, but it is dangerous and can easily spill on you—or, worse, the person you are interviewing with! Have something to drink beforehand so you can focus 100% on your interviewer.

- Taking extensive notes, and not paying enough attention to what is being said. Sometimes an attempt to make yourself look attentive and on-the-ball can backfire and just make you seem detached and unengaged. Make sure your focus is on the person with whom you are actually speaking.

- Getting too comfortable with the person you are interviewing with. Some people become too casual and can often reveal inappropriate information, and a too-casual attitude from the start can give the impression that you don not respect the workplace where you are applying.

- Focusing on the negative. Do not share all the reasons your prior positions did not work or what you did not like about past employers. Businesses are looking for positive people who get along well with others and their employers.

- Bringing too much stuff into the interview with you. Being prepared is good, but it is unnecessary to bring more than one bag or notebook. Carrying around a lot of things makes you look cluttered and disorganized—or like you have something more important to do later.

- Not bringing enough! Always have an extra copy or two of your resume, and make sure to bring pen and paper for if you do get important information that you need to write down.

- Talking too much! Nobody likes a chatterbox who does not let the other person speak—and that includes your interviewer.

- Having a dead-fish handshake. No one wants to hire someone who is not confident enough to have a strong handshake (the bone-cruncher handshake is just as bad).

- Showing up late. Enough said.

## COMMON QUESTIONS

Some interviewers take pride in writing all of their questions themselves, and others just take a list out of a book. There is no way of knowing exactly what you will be asked, and because you are different from every other job seeker out there, there is no "right answer" to any of them. However, it can be very useful to study the questions most commonly asked by interviewers. Keep in mind the principles we've talked about, and try to come up with answers for these which are true to yourself and would impress a potential employer:

Tell me about yourself.

Why should we want to hire you?

Why would you like to work for us?

Why did you leave your last job/Why are you looking to leave your job?

What is your biggest weakness/strength?

What is your bottom line salary requirement or what are your salary expectations?

What makes you qualified for this job?

What do you know about this company?

What can you contribute to this company?

Are you overqualified for this position?

What motivates you?

What has been your biggest disappointment in life?

What was the biggest challenge/failure or success you have ever faced/achieved?

How do you handle pressure/stress?

Tell me about a time when you didn't get along with your boss and how you handled it.

What type of work environment do you prefer?

Do you prefer to work independently or as part of a team?

Describe a time where you encountered a problem on a project and how you overcame it.

Where do you see yourself in five years?

What are you looking for in your next position?

How do you plan to achieve those goals?

There is no way to know for sure which questions you will be asked, and every individual's answers will be different, but the key is to remember to stay on message! Turn every question around to highlight how you will be valuable to the company.

## THE WEAKNESS QUESTION

"What is your greatest weakness?" is one of those questions that seem to worry people a great deal. It is sort of a head game, since it blatantly asks you to describe something negative about yourself.

I once coached a job seeker who was about to go into her interview and tell the interviewer that her biggest weakness was that she stayed up late each night with worry about what the attorneys would think of her, causing her to come in late to work in the morning! Whatever you say your biggest weakness is, make sure you can turn it around into something that is actually a positive.

Here is how I train people to approach "the weakness question." Essentially, whatever your personal weakness is, you need to follow this formula: "What could be considered a weakness is X because of Y and Z. However, because of A and B it can also be a positive."

It is important not to say something that points to a definite weakness, such as saying "My weakness is . . ." Instead, you want to articulate how something "could" be considered a potential weakness. You can use this formula with almost any weakness you might think of for yourself. Let's say you have a tendency to take on too many projects at once. You can say: "What could be considered a weakness is that I often take on too many projects at once. Some people might see this as a weakness because I could spread myself too thin, but what I have found is that a lot of my peers appreciate the fact that I am always willing to take on extra work. They really admire my ability to keep so many balls in the air at the same time. In addition, I have found ways to better manage my time so that I can take on more projects in a day and have learned to delegate when necessary to achieve positive outcomes on multiple projects simultaneously."

## BEHAVIORAL QUESTIONS

The questions above are fairly standard ones, and once you know them it is usually fairly obvious what you should be on the lookout for. But there is another kind of question that is more personal and can often present more of a challenge. A behavioral question is one that asks how you did or would behave given a certain situation.

There is not much you can do to prepare for a behavioral interview. One tip I can give you that can enhance your chances of success in a behavioral interview is to, as **homework**, *come up with a list of at least ten situations, including times where you overcame an obstacle or challenge, and how those situations were resolved.*

Following is a list of some of the more common behavioral interview questions:

Tell me about how you worked effectively under pressure.

Describe a situation in which you were able to use persuasion to successfully convince someone to see things your way.

Describe a time when you were faced with a stressful situation that demonstrated your coping skills.

Give me an example of a time when you set a goal and were able to meet or achieve it.

Give me a specific example of a time when you had to conform to a policy with which you did not agree.

Please discuss an important written document you were required to complete.

Tell me about a time when you had to go above and beyond the call of duty in order to get a job done.

Describe a situation when you or a group that you were a part of were in danger of missing a deadline. What did you do?

Give me an example of a time when you had to make a split-second decision.

Give me an example of a bad decision that you made and what you learned from that mistake.

Tell me about a time when something you tried to accomplish failed. What did you learn from that failure?

Tell me about a time when you had too many things to do and you were required to prioritize your tasks.

What is your typical way of dealing with conflict? Give me an example.

Tell me about a time you were able to successfully deal with another person even when that individual may not have personally liked you (or vice versa).

Give me an example of when you showed initiative and took the lead.

Tell me about a recent situation in which you had to deal with a very upset customer or coworker.

Give me an example of a time when you used your fact-finding skills to solve a problem.

Tell me about a time when you missed an obvious solution to a problem.

Describe a time when you anticipated potential problems and developed preventive measures.

Tell me about a time when you were forced to make an unpopular decision.

Have you handled a difficult situation with a coworker? How?

What do you do when your schedule is interrupted? Give an example of how you handle it.

Tell me about a time when you delegated a project effectively.

Have you gone above and beyond the call of duty? If so, how?

Describe a decision you made that was unpopular and how you handled implementing it.

Give me an example of a goal you reached and tell me how you achieved it.

Give me an example of an occasion when you used logic to solve a problem.

## TRICK QUESTIONS

There are several interview questions that are meant to trick you, and these questions require a little creative thinking. One such example is: "What sort of management style do you prefer: someone who micro-manages you or someone who gives you complete autonomy?"

This trick question forces the candidate to pick a side. The average job candidate would choose one option over the other and then make a case for their decision. A top-notch job candidate would think outside the box, and perhaps answer "Both."

The trick to answering these difficult questions is to come up with a third option. The third option could sound something like this:

"I am looking to find a position where I can build a trusting relationship with whatever manager I wind up working for. I realize that trust is something that you have to earn, so I would expect that in the beginning I might need a little more guidance and direction. As time goes on, I hope to create a mutual understanding and a symbiotic relationship built on clear communication. As I gain more experience, I would hope the manager I work for would begin to give me more flexibility and to trust in my judgment."

This is just one example of how you can transform an either/or question into an opportunity to create something new. This method works with a variety of different situational questions. It is important never to leave the person you are interviewing with on the defensive. You always want to address the question that is being asked and come up with a creative solution that works for everyone.

## SHOULD YOU MENTION MEDICAL ISSUES?

A lot of job seekers are unclear as to whether they should mention that they were out on disability or had to take time off for a medical issue. My recommendation is that you stay away from any conversations about medical leave, medical procedures or disability. You are better off saying you had a personal matter to attend to or something similar as the term "personal matter" does not typically have the same negative connotation as a medical matter or issue.

The reason you want to stay clear of these topics in an interview is that an employer could potentially use that information to discriminate against you. Legally they are not supposed to discriminate, but that does not mean that they won't.

An employer is not allowed to legally ask you any questions about your medical history so there is no reason you should go out of your way to disclose that information unnecessarily.

So how should you handle it if you have taken some time off for a medical leave or medical procedure?

I would recommend saying something to the effect of "I really enjoyed working for my last employer (start with what you liked about your last position); however, I had some personal matters that I had to attend to that required me to take time off for an extended period."

Most employers will be OK with this type of an answer. Some might push you further by asking "what personal issues?" but most will not because of the legalities around pushing for more information.

If you have the choice, it is simply more helpful not to plant the idea that you might lose your new employer time and resources with a future medical problem. Like ageism, this is a form of discrimination that is unfortunate, but a fact of life with some of the people you will have to deal with.

## DO NOT TELL TOO MUCH

If you can effectively communicate that you can do the job and that you have the right skills and can fit in, then the job is yours. So why do most people not get hired?

What people often do in the interview is *give* employers reasons not to hire them. The average person has the right skills and could do the job, but they share inappropriate information during the interview. The following are examples of inappropriate things to discuss in an interview that will cause the employer to not want to hire you.

1. Sharing medical information, such as the fact that you were on a recent medical leave.

2. Sharing information that is personal, such as the fact that you are divorced and going through a hard time.

3. Sharing information that is covered under the federal discrimination laws (EEOC), such as information related to your age, race, sexual orientation, etc.

4. Complaining about past employers and exhibiting a negative attitude about anything in general.

5. Sharing confidential information about your past employer that is not meant for public knowledge.

These are just a few examples of things you could discuss that would give employers a reason not to hire you.

Keep this in mind in your next interview and remember to use discretion!

## SO WHAT IS MISSING?

If you are reading this book, there is a possibility you have already spent some time looking for a job. But the fact that you are reading this book also means you probably have not found it yet—or that if you have you are not completely happy with it.

What is missing? Why is it that some people seem to have all the luck finding jobs? What are the key contributing factors that differentiate those who get hired from those who do not?

Three key components contribute to a job seeker's effectiveness at landing the job they want. These three components are the same three components that can make an attorney effective at winning a case. If any one of these components is missing, you will NOT making the strongest case for why an employer should hire you.

The first component that leads an attorney to be successful at making the strongest case for their client is the number one reason people do not get hired when they go in for an interview: a lack of proper preparation. A few years ago you could get away without being properly prepared because there were an abundance of open jobs. Now that the market has shifted and there are more people looking than jobs available, you really have to bring your A-game if you expect to get an offer. Spend at least thirty minutes to an hour researching the company and the position before you go for your interview.

The second component that makes an attorney effective in winning a case is integrity. A major reason why job seekers do not get hired or get passed on is because they misrepresent their skills, education and/or work history on their resume (no integrity). More and more we are noticing people who "inflate" their skills, add a fake degree and/or increase their length of time at their last employer on their resume. The sad thing is, for the most part, they do not have to go to such extreme lengths to get hired. Many times these job seekers would be hired based on their real skill set or resume, if only they would not lie.

If you are worried that your resume might not represent you effectively, do not resort to lying! Instead, work with a recruiter, career coach or resume writer to see how you can represent your background in a better light. I have represented many people who have been out of work for two or more years or who have been light on certain skills and yet I am still able to find them jobs by teaching them to be honest and coaching them on how to represent their backgrounds more effectively.

The third component that leads an attorney be effective in trial, and which you as a job seeker need to be conscious of, is evidence. No attorney has ever won a case without providing strong evidence to support their client's claims. The same is true of you as a job seeker. Many job seekers go to an interview unprepared, and have no evidence for why that employer should hire them.

Although these three components (preparation, integrity and evidence) are the main reasons people do not get the job offer, there is one more critical element to the interview that can cause the job seeker not to be hired. This last element is a lack of professionalism in the interview. This can mean the way you dress, the way you act and/or your overall appearance and demeanor. I had someone go in for an interview where she looked at her reflection in the window during the duration of the interview. I have also had job seekers who just have a bad attitude who get passed on and also have seen many people lose job offers over something as simple as not wearing a suit.

Now, these are pretty simple rules. If you follow them all well, you are bound to see greater success. Are there more important details? Of course! That's what the rest of the book is for.

## IF YOU WERE LAID OFF

What does it mean about you if you were laid off? Does it mean that you are not employable or that there is something wrong with you? Absolutely not! People who have been laid off are getting hired all the time. The layoff is not what matters. What matters is how you handle your explanation of being laid off in the interview.

I meet with hundreds, if not thousands, of job seekers every year. In the past two years a large number of these job seekers have been people who were laid off. Many of them ask me what they are doing wrong that is resulting in them not landing the job. I share with them that they are not doing anything wrong; it is just that they are not being effective in their explanation of why they left their last position.

When I ask someone why they left their last position often they will give me an incredulous look that says "duh!," and then they will say some version of the following: "I was laid off," "My company closed," "My position was eliminated," etc. *Do not focus on the layoff!*

The problem is that everyone is saying the same thing and that is *not* memorable. What I coach my clients to do is to focus on what they liked about their last job, rather than focusing on the layoff, and then to follow up with how excited they are to find a great new position they can stay at long term. For example, if Betty was at her company five years and she loved her job, I would have Betty start by telling the employer why she stayed at her job for five years and how much she enjoyed her job. Then I would coach Betty to lightly mention the layoff, and finish by focusing on what she gets to create in her next position.

As a counterexample, I worked with one woman who when asked why she left her last job at a law office replied that all the other girls were jealous of her and thought she was having sex with all of the attorneys—because she was. If the short skirt and knee-high clubbing boots she wore did not lose her the job that line did!

## SKELETONS IN THE CLOSET

There is a little mantra that I teach people to help them to remember this for their interview. I call it the GOOD-BAD-GOOD method. Next time you get stuck on a tricky question that could come across as negative in an interview, always try to start with a positive, lightly touch on the negative aspect, and then finish by bringing it back to a positive. You want to highlight your advantages as an employee, not focus attention on a time when a company found you expendable.

This technique should work for any unflattering fact that might come up with a potential employer, with a few exceptions. Criminal history will show up on a background check, and many employers will forgive one DUI but not more, or not other types of infractions. As this tends to be policy, there is little that can be done about it apart from giving a full disclosure when asked. Being proven a liar only makes you look worse.

As clichéd as it may sound, honesty is the best policy where potentially damaging information is concerned—you want to put a good spin on the truth rather than hiding it completely.

I once had a client ask me to place his daughter with a temp job, which I did. Unfortunately she was fired after getting nauseous and becoming sick during her first week. It turned out she was pregnant and did not want anybody to know. We had to cover to make the situation look good, but any problems could have been avoided with some honesty at the beginning.

## WHAT ABOUT IF YOU WERE TERMINATED?

Getting fired is never easy. Many people will be terminated for one reason or another at some point in their career, but I have noticed in speaking with a lot of the unemployed that they are confused about what constitutes a "layoff" versus a "termination." Many job seekers are going into an interview saying they were terminated, when that is not the case.

In recent years, many people have been laid off due to the economy. Typically a layoff is something that happens when a company has to make cutbacks for whatever reason.

The term "termination" is most often used to describe when someone has been let go for cause. Being terminated for cause means that you did something that caused the company to have to terminate you. Examples of reasons someone would be terminated for cause are as follows:

- Sharing trade secrets or confidential information
- Violating a company policy
- Stealing

- Constantly being late or missing too much work
- Making too many mistakes
- Etc.

A layoff often happens because:

- A company is cutting staff
- A company is relocating
- A company is restructuring

It is important to be clear whether you were laid off or terminated. Even if you were terminated, I would not recommend using the word "termination" to describe your reason for leaving, such as saying "I was terminated." The word termination has a very negative connotation in our culture.

A former employer will never say you were terminated either. They can only confirm your dates of hire, salary and, in some cases, whether you are eligible for rehire. A potential employer might be able to infer that you were terminated if a company says that you are not eligible for rehire, but beyond that most companies will not specifically say that you were terminated.

If you were terminated and have to explain why you left your last position, you might want to try saying, "We came to a mutual decision that it was not the right fit," or something similar that conveys that you and the company came to a decision for you to part ways.

Being asked directly if you were terminated is very different than being asked why you left your last position. If you are asked directly on an application or by an employer whether you ever have been terminated, you have to be 100% honest at all times and state yes if you have been terminated.

Whether you were "laid off" or "terminated," you always want to be sure to use the GOOD-BAD-GOOD method in explaining why you left your last position.

Henry was terminated from his last position due to a personality conflict with a new boss. He is asked in an interview why he left his most recent position. He responds using the GOOD-BAD-GOOD method, "I was very excited when I originally accepted the position. The company had a great reputation and the work was exactly what I wanted to be doing. Shortly after I started with the company, my direct boss left and was replaced with someone who I had not worked with before. The environment changed and I eventually decided it was not a place I saw myself staying long term, so we came to a mutual decision that I would pursue other opportunities. This worked out for the best, because after I left I have been temping and have gained a lot of new skills that I would not otherwise have learned that I can apply to my new endeavors."

Always start with the GOOD (why you originally accepted the position and why you stayed there as long as you did), then lightly touch on the BAD (why the layoff or termination happened), and finally follow up with the GOOD (what you intend to create out of leaving your most recent position, that is, what is next for you).

Stay away from saying things like "it was not my choice," "it was unfair," etc. Instead, look at how you can find the positive in all of this and convey your positive attitude in the interview regardless of your circumstances.

## THE PHONE INTERVIEW

In many cases, especially when you are applying for a job in another town or to work for a company remotely, you will be asked to give a telephone interview. This can be more difficult because neither you nor your interviewer can see the other person, but the important thing to remember is to treat it just as if you were being interviewed in person— your attitude *does* show through in your telephone manner.

In that sense, your preparation should be largely the same, but I have prepared a useful list of dos and don'ts to get you ready before the big call.

## DO:

- Stand up and smile during your phone interview. Energy and positive attitude come through much stronger in your voice when your body language projects them. Remember: The physical shape that our bodies and faces make affect the way we produce sounds and form words—and your interviewer will be able to hear this.

- Have your resume and a list of accomplishments nearby for reference. You can "cheat" much more in a phone interview, so it is useful to have some materials at hand to glance at when you need to generate ideas.

- Speak on a landline. Cell phones are much more prone to bad connections and interference, as we have all experienced. If you and the interviewer cannot hear each other, it helps no one.

- Research a company just as you would for a normal interview. Just because you do not have to be there does not mean you should be one iota less prepared. This will assist you in exactly the same way.

- Have a pen and paper and a glass of water handy. You will be speaking a lot, and you may go over important information that you will want to save—especially if, for instance, you need to make an appointment for a second interview! Do not get caught unprepared to take down information or by losing your voice mid-interview.

- Speak slowly and clearly, and give short concise answers! When you cannot see your interviewer, it is that much harder to pick up on it if you are boring your interviewer or being unclear. Take extra precautions so that you are not.

## DON'T:

- Interrupt the interviewer! People often naturally run over each other's speech in person or with friends, but, again, speaking over the phone gives us fewer cues and less information to work with. Interrupting just comes off as rude over the telephone (and usually in person!).

- Have any noise in the background (pets and children included). Do not sound like you just squeezed in time for the interview in between errands. Noise in the background is also distracting and makes it harder to hear *you*, which is the point. Set aside time in a quiet indoor location.

- Have too much clutter distracting you, read from your resume or from pre-written answers, or pretend that you know something that you do not or Google search while on the call. If you are doing something else or lying on the telephone, it *will* be noticeable in your voice, and you will not sound good. If you don't know an answer, talk about how that's something you're excited to learn about. If you are convincing enough that nobody can tell when you are playing solitaire or Googling answers rather than paying attention, then maybe you should be at a Hollywood audition rather than a job interview!

- Chew or eat anything while on the call. This is extremely easy to hear, and makes you sound like you barely found the time to speak with your future employer—as well as making your speech indistinct. Not a good impression.

- Bring up salary or benefits. Discuss this delicately in person later!

- Forget to send a "thank you" letter and/or email because it is a phone screen. The person you spoke with still spent just as much of their time speaking with you. Don't neglect to show them that you appreciate it.

## THE DREADED THREESOME

Panel interviews are typically twice as hard and half as much fun as regular interviews. Instead of trying to capture the attention of one cranky human resources professional, you are now responsible for entertaining two, three or sometimes even five interviewers at once. But they keep coming up, so job seekers like yourself will have to deal with them. The question then becomes, how do you keep their attention in a positive manner?

It all comes down to sticking with the basic principles that work in one-on-one interviews, but making some important modifications.

One suggestion I would make is to periodically address each interviewer by name. A job seeker recently shared a story with me, wherein she perceived that the interview did not go as well as she had hoped. One of the three people interviewing her seemed to be completely disinterested and practically ignored her. She asked me what she could have done differently, and I gave her the following advice. Take the time to address each person by name and focus on each individual as you are speaking.

If Interviewer A, let's call him Bob, is not giving you the time of day, then it is time to take more drastic measures. Bob may have other things on his mind, but you can quickly bring him back to earth and help him focus on what is important: YOU!

One method to draw an interviewer into focus is to direct a statement to the person whose attention you would like to capture, for example: "Bob, let me share with you some interesting ideas and strategies about X that I feel I could bring to the table."

Bob's lackadaisical attitude may have nothing to do with you; therefore, it is critical not to take it personally. You should always maintain your enthusiasm, as well as a positive attitude.

It is important to be intentional in your speaking at all times; however, in "the dreaded threesome" or another panel situation, it is even more critical to be focused and engaged with each individual, especially if one seems aloof. All great speakers know that you have to speak to each person in the audience as if you were speaking with them one-on-one. The more eye contact and focus you have, the stronger your panel interview will come across!

## DO I NEED TO ASK QUESTIONS AT THE END?

One of the most overlooked pieces of an interview is the opportunity for you to ask the potential employer questions about the job. The two places where you can leave the most lasting impression on the interviewer are how you start the interview and how you finish it. When you reach the end of the interview and the interviewer asks you: "Do you have any questions for me?" it is imperative that you have questions readily available. Not just any questions either, but good questions. If you do not have questions prepared, the interviewer may think that you are not interested in the position. So what are good questions? I have several of my favorite questions that I recommend to ask which I share with you below. Additionally, I have started discussions in various forums to see what other people felt were good questions. "Give me three words to describe the company culture," was a question shared with me by the VP of HR of a major corporation. It is his favorite question to be asked at the end of an interview and can often give the person insight into the company.

My favorite questions to ask at the end of an interview are:

- *"What sort of ramp-up period do you expect for someone coming into this position?"*
- *"What qualities does your ideal candidate possess and how do you see me fitting into those parameters?"*
- *"Of the people who have had this position in the past, what have you found worked most effectively about those individuals and what, if any, were the areas that you would have liked to have seen improvement in?"*
- *"What has been your biggest challenge with filling this position?"*
- *"What is it that you like about working for XYZ company?"*
- *"What is the biggest obstacle that someone will face coming into this position?"*

Additional questions shared with me from various discussions include the following:

- *"What are the primary goals you see for the individual you hire for this role to meet in order to be successful—in other words, what are the challenges that currently exist that need to be dealt with first and foremost?"* This gives you an opportunity to expound on how you could go about dealing with those challenges or how you've dealt with similar challenges in the past.
- *"I'm excited about the potential within this position and particularly with XYZ company. What are your next steps in the interview process?"* You need to know what to expect next.
- *"What is your leadership style?"*
- *"What are your communication preferences (i.e., email, voicemail, text, IM, cell, in-person, etc.)?"*
- *"What are the learning goals you would like your team to accomplish (i.e., technical proficiency, current expense policy, in-house intranet, etc.)?"*

My favorite way to end an interview is by using something similar to this statement/question:

"Thank you for giving me an opportunity to meet with you. I really enjoyed learning more about the position and the company. After discussing my qualifications, are there any concerns or hesitations that you have about my background that we have not already covered?"

This gives you an opportunity to address any areas that you may not have discussed previously in the interview.

## BREAKING DOWN YOUR SALARY

A lot of job seekers do not realize the importance of knowing their salary and how to break it down to a potential employer in an interview. Whether you are working with a recruiter or applying directly with a company, it is your responsibility to clearly communicate your current salary. If this is not clearly communicated to the employer or recruiter during the interview process and/or on the application, you can easily have your offer rescinded if the numbers do not match up.

Example: If you tell a potential employer that you make $65,000 a year, when in reality you have a base of $60,000, a bonus of $3,000 and $2,000 worth of overtime, you can have your offer rescinded when the employer or recruiter goes to verify this information.

The way to avoid this is to clearly break down your salary on the application into Base + Bonus + OT + any additional benefits that might be monetary in nature such as 401k or profit sharing contribution.

Not every application gives room to break this all down, so in a worst-case scenario, only list your base salary and then clearly explain if/when asked the breakdown of your salary in more detail, but *do not* just lump everything together on an application without a clear breakdown. By doing this you will avoid any confusion regarding your compensation and will ensure your offer is secure once it is made to you.

## WHAT IF I NEED TO CANCEL?

Is it ever appropriate to cancel an interview and if so, how should you go about doing it without burning your bridges?

It is not suggested that you go around canceling interviews that you set up for yourself or that your recruiter sets up for you, but there are occasions where it may be appropriate to cancel your interview. Often you are not familiar with a company until you begin to research them prior to your initial interview.

Remember, when you research a company prior to any interview you should come up with at least five reasons why you want to work for the company, five reasons why the company should want to hire you and five questions regarding the position. If you cannot think of five strong reasons why they might want to work for this employer, then the position might not be worth going in for an interview. I respect and appreciate the job seeker who gets in touch with me early to let me know the position might not be the right fit for them.

A perfect example illustrating this occurred with a job seeker who I was preparing for an executive assistant interview supporting the CEO of a major Fortune 500 company. In doing her research, she found out that the company invested in lab space. She was an avid animal rights activist and did not feel comfortable working at a company where the company invested in space where animals would be tested. She immediately contacted me to let me know. She asked me if I would like her to still go on the interview or if we should cancel. I respected her for doing her research and not wasting the company's time or mine. I proceeded to cancel her interview, save the relationship with the company and get her a position with a different company a few weeks later.

Employers and recruiters appreciate it when you are honest with them and do not go to an interview just for the sake of going. We know your time is valuable and appreciate it when you show us the same respect for our time. There have been several occasions throughout my career where a job seeker has researched a company and realized that the position is not in line with their "Wishlist." Typically, my client will appreciate their honesty, and will not hold it against them if another position comes up down the road that might be a better fit. If you know you do not plan to accept a position, the employer will appreciate your saving them time by skipping the interview, and should not be compelled to blackball you in any way.

If you do intend to cancel an interview, please do try to give your recruiter or potential employer ample notice. There might be occasions where it is acceptable to cancel an interview, but always keep in mind, once you cancel the interview the first time, you might not be able to get a second interview.

## TEN THINGS THAT SEPARATE THE WHEAT FROM THE CHAFF

Finally, while you keep in mind all that you have learned about the interview, let's review the ten vital keys that in my experience mark the line between the two most important categories at interviews: those who get hired and those who do not.

So why does one person get hired over another? Do you get the interviews, but never get the offers? There are people getting hired in this tough economy, so the question becomes, how do you make yourself stand out from the other people who are also looking for a job?

People who get hired . . .

1. Research a firm thoroughly before their interviews, and create a persuasive case for why they should be the one chosen for the position.

2. Exhibit self-confidence and can provide at least ten examples of where they will increase the company's PEP (productivity, effectiveness and performance).

3. Have a minimum of ten talking points prepared that support the case for why they should be hired and consistently utilize these points throughout the interview to solidify their position.

4. Drive by the location of the interview in advance so that they will not get lost the day of the interview.

5. Give themselves an extra thirty minutes or more to account for traffic, arrive early and review their notes before they go in.

6. Keep in touch with good contacts at their prior companies so that it is easy to provide outstanding references when requested.

7. Fill out their application thoroughly and completely and never put "see attached resume" on their application.

8. Practice their interview questions and answers with a professional coach or a friend who is willing to be brutally honest regarding their response.

9. Prepare and give a great "Tell me about yourself" that addresses the company's problem and how they intend to solve it.

10. Never put the interviewer on the defensive, including exhibiting a flexible attitude throughout the entire interview.

...and they always dress to impress!

Keep the principles I have outlined in mind, and you should find yourself getting job offers after your interviews much sooner rather than later or not at all.

# 7 | After the Interview

*"Dare to live the life you have dreamed for yourself. Go forward and make your dreams come true."*
*Ralph Waldo Emerson*

## THE ART OF THE THANK YOU CARD

Job seekers ask me whether they should send a "thank you" letter following their interview. The answer is always YES! I highly recommend sending at least one, if not two, "thank you" letters. Ideally, you should send one "thank you" letter via email the same day as your interview, and a handwritten "thank you" letter the next day.

I have shared an article on Facebook about how important "thank you" letters are, and how underutilized they are in today's market. One of my clients saw the article and shared it with her social network stating that, "In the ten plus years that I have been in human resources, I have only ever received three 'thank you' letters." She went on to say that she still remembers each of those individuals who sent her a "thank you" note to this day.

The following is an example of what a "thank you" letter should look like.

Dear Mr. Employer,

I would like to thank you for taking time out of your busy schedule to meet with me this week regarding your job opportunity. I enjoyed learning more about both you and the organization. I strongly feel that my background in (insert your specialty here) would make me a great asset to your organization. I look forward to seeing you again, and to pursuing this opportunity further.

Sincerely,
A. Job Seeker

Keep it short, sweet and to the point. I would encourage you to modify it and make it your own or come up with your own version that expresses you.

Now, how hard was that? Really, people—a thank you letter does not have to be complicated! The most important thing is to send one and to make sure you proofread it! I cannot tell you how many business executives and human resources professionals I have worked with who complain about not receiving a simple thank you letter or worse, have complained about unprofessional or poorly written thank you letters.

Do you have to handwrite one? No. However, I would strongly encourage you to do so. The reason that you want to send a handwritten note in addition to an email one is to go the extra mile. What gets a person hired is proving they are willing to go above and beyond, and writing a handwritten thank you letter is the best way to do so.

You initially want to send an email "thank you" letter with just the basics, as I have shown above. Thank them for their time, remind them why you would be an asset and let them know you are interested in following up on the position. This email "thank you" letter should be sent the day of the interview so that you are on their mind at the end of that day or the beginning of the next. Then, you want to write and mail a handwritten "thank you" letter the following day. Thus they will receive your handwritten "thank you" letter a few days after the interview, and will again be reminded to think of you.

Follow these two easy steps:

1. Send an email thank you letter the day of the interview.
2. Send a follow-up handwritten thank you letter the day after the interview.

There are many different ways to follow up. You could follow up with a phone call after an interview or you could follow up with your potential boss on an important matter so that they do not forget. I cannot tell you how many times one form of strong follow-up or another has gotten someone hired. If you are going to follow up with a phone call after an interview, it is important that you follow up once and not ten times.

You do *not* want to come across as too pushy, but you *do* want to come across as interested in the position. It is a fine line, but an important one. I have some people who call my office twenty times a day or so asking if I have anything for them. This does not endear me to those job seekers. Unless you are doing something like that, you do not need to worry about being too pushy! Polite follow-ups are not only acceptable but expected, and timely.

You will be guaranteed to stay fresh in the minds of your potential employers.

## SO YOU HAVE GOTTEN A JOB OFFER

I am confident that if you follow the advice that I have laid out in this book, you should find yourself in fulfilling employment in a short amount of time. This does not mean that it is time to abandon the lessons you have learned. As soon as you receive the offer there are more decisions to be made and the best way to keep a job is to behave as if you are continually applying for it!

It is important that we address some important questions that will come up once you have secured a job offer.

### Should you negotiate on salary?

In these tough economic times, I am finding that a lot of clients are getting lowballed when offer time comes around. The question then becomes: Should I lower my salary requirements and accept an offer for less than I am worth?

The answer is, be flexible and carefully evaluate all your options. The most important thing is to be the one to get the job offer! Whether the offer comes in 5k, 10k or 20k less than what you want is irrelevant. When you receive an offer, you are ahead of the game. You do not have much power to negotiate upfront, but once a company has set its sights on you and have chosen to give *you* the offer, you are in a much better position to negotiate.

You have to ask yourself, "What is my bottom line?" Perhaps you were making 100k before, and now you get an offer for 90k. Is 90k something you can live on, and more importantly, are you going to have the opportunity to get back to where you were within a year or two? Something most talented employees know is that they determine their own worth. You might get lowballed initially, but if you know that you can prove your worth you will be rewarded in the long run.

One of the women I interviewed explained that she once took a position paying 30k a year, but knew that there was enormous upside potential. She saw the value in the company and what she could contribute, and within eight months was making close to 700k. Now, this may not be the norm, but it goes to show that you can do a lot with the cards you are dealt.

Remember, the next time you get an offer that is less than what you want, ask yourself what is the upside potential? If the money is below what is absolutely necessary, then perhaps you need to renegotiate or turn it down. If instead you realize that there is a large upside and you can negotiate a review in 60–90 days or possibly even six months, then it might be wise to seriously consider it.

Sometimes negotiation is almost a necessity. I once had a client come in with an offer of $52,500 for a person who was currently making $54,000 and wanted $65,000. An offer like that looked absurd at its face value, even if it is in a field that you are more interested in. It is hard to voluntarily take that kind of pay cut, but it was better to barter a little then shut the door on the offer. The company came back with a better offer of $60,000 and she ended up taking the job!

## Negotiating your salary

So let's say you have decided to negotiate on salary. How do you go about doing it?

Have you ever received an offer that you were dissatisfied with? If you did, it is probably because you were not coming from a position of power in the negotiation process. It is a recruiter's job to eliminate that variable, as their goal is to negotiate the best offer possible on your behalf. However, when you apply to a job on your own, you are responsible for negotiating your own salary. So how do you do it?

The most important thing to note is to *never* list a number when it says on the application what is your desired salary. The moment you write a specific number down or verbally give a specific figure, you have essentially eliminated any room for negotiation. Always write "negotiable" or "flexible" on the application or when asked verbally for your salary requirements, let the employer know you are "open to any fair offer" or, if pushed for a number, give a range such as low to mid 80s.

I once worked with a pair of sisters who had had exactly the same work history since leaving college, and were applying at the same company again. One listed her desired salary as "negotiable" and the other listed $53,000. Sure enough, the one was offered $58,000 and the other got her "desired salary" of $53,000!

Listing specific numbers can never help you since going too low will limit what kind of an offer you get (potentially losing you thousands per year!), and going too high can only eventually price you out of the market. I once had an employer tell me that they were giving a candidate what was normally a $75,000 job, but since she had listed $60,000 as her desired salary, that was what she was getting. She still has the job and that may be what she still makes at it!

Let's say you get an offer of $80,000/year, with a 10% discretionary bonus and full benefits. You are currently earning $78,000 a year with a similar bonus and you were hoping for at least a $5,000 increase to make a move. How do you handle it once you receive the offer?

The first thing you have to ask yourself is: Am I willing to walk away from this offer? If you are, then you are in a very powerful negotiating position. However, if you are not, then you have some serious thinking to do. Are you willing to risk losing the offer over a few thousand dollars?

If you do believe that you deserve to make that extra few thousand dollars, you have to be able to justify why you are worth it. A few things you can use as negotiating points to justify why you deserve to make the extra money are as follows:

- How many years of experience do you have in the business?
- How do the benefits compare to your current benefits?
- Do you have any specialized skills, qualifications or advanced degrees that make you more qualified than another candidate?
- What is the industry standard compensation for the position you are applying for with your level of experience?

Next, if you are willing to walk away from the offer, then you should be direct and let them know once the offer is extended what your bottom line that you are willing to accept is and why you feel you are entitled to that level of an increase using the above listed negotiating points.

If, however, you are unwilling to risk the possibility of losing the offer you currently have, but still want to see if there is wiggle room, I would suggest the following script.

"Thank you very much for your generous offer of $80,000 a year. I really appreciate the opportunity to work for your company. In a perfect world, I was hoping to be closer to $83,000 a year given my years of experience and qualifications. Is this a firm offer or is there any possibility of getting me to my stated goal of $83,000 a year?"

Typically you will get one of two responses:

A. No, there is no room for negotiation.

B. There might be, let me check.

If you get the first response, you can then go to a default plan and see if there is the possibility of a review after 90 or 180 days for an increase. Otherwise, you will have to determine if you can live with that offer. If you get the second response then you should be patient and see what they come back with as a counteroffer.

## Avoiding the rescinded job offer

There are few things more frustrating than having what you want dangled in front of you only to have it taken away. Once you get the offer you should not be afraid to feel some well-earned relief, but there are a few simple steps you should make sure you have taken so that your new company is not forced to take back its offer.

1. Always advise your recruiter or potential employer if you may have any misdemeanors or other potential issues with your background check in *advance*.

2. Always cross-check your employments dates and only list months if required on your resume. If your months are off even slightly this can have your offer rescinded.

3. If you started a job "temp" but it went permanent, you would want to be sure to clarify what dates were temp and what dates were permanent.

4. Make sure any education listed on your resume is verifiable and/ or that you can provide an authentic copy of your degree or of the certificate that you have listed.

5. DO NOT LIE. This is a good catchall to avoid getting your offer rescinded and covers all of the above topics.

If you lie about anything, no matter how insignificant or small it may seem, an employer has every right to rescind your job offer. Get the job offer on your own merits and do not give the employer that opportunity to rescind the offer. The bottom line is to be responsible for what you are putting out there—and if you cannot verify something, leave it out! This includes not only your educational qualifications and the dates of your employment history, but your salary as well. Be honest, and use how you talk about something to make it sound better; do not change the facts as they stand.

Yahoo! CEO Scott Thompson had to leave the company after it turned out that he had had inaccurate information on his resume. If something like that can come back to bite someone as powerful as him, it is certainly not something you want hanging over your own head!

## Buying time with multiple offers

A recent occurrence that we have been seeing is a job seeker getting multiple offers at once. This is a great trend in the market because it is an indicator that the economy is improving, but it comes with a downside: Many job seekers have no idea how to effectively handle more than one offer at a time. We are seeing a lot of job seekers lose offers because they are mismanaging their communication with both the company who is giving them the offer and the recruiter who got it for them.

When you have more than one offer, the most important thing to keep in mind is CLEAR COMMUNICATION.

When you start trying to buy yourself time by not responding to a company or to a recruiter, you are jeopardizing your potential offers. If you are in the final stages with any company, law firm or recruiter, you need to be an open book when it comes to your other offers or pending opportunities. Most companies and recruiters will understand. It is important that you return phone calls and emails promptly when you are in the offer stage with any company. You are better off to respond immediately explaining your situation, than to wait too long and lose the offer.

I once had a job seeker who got one offer from her first interview, but still had three other interviews to go on that week. We clearly communicated this to each of the companies and they were very understanding. They allowed her to go on all of the interviews and the first company appreciated her honesty and was willing to wait for her so that she could fairly assess each opportunity. In the end, she had four offers; however, she went with the first one who had patiently waited for her. If she had lied to the first company or been evasive regarding her other interviews, she could have easily lost the best offer she had.

Just remember, be in communication. It is better to let the company know that you are in the final stage with another company and ask if they are OK with waiting for you to see through the process than lying about it. If you do this you will be respected and taken more seriously.

## Handling a counteroffer

What is a counteroffer and how can you effectively handle it when you receive one?

A counteroffer occurs when the company that you are currently working for does not accept your resignation and offers to match or better the offer with the new company that you have received the offer through.

Many companies have strict policies on not giving counteroffers, as they know that it is rare for a counteroffer to be successful, while others will stop at nothing to keep their best employees. So is it a good idea to accept a counteroffer once you have already accepted a new position?

Of the many job seekers who I have placed and coached throughout the years, only a few have ever accepted a counteroffer and chose to stay with their original employer for more than six months.

Why is it that most job seekers do not stay when they do accept a counteroffer from their current employer?

1. There were certain reasons that you were looking for a new position to begin with and typically, a company will promise to "fix" those issues, but in reality, you still wind up dealing with the same issues that they were originally faced with because companies cannot change their culture.

2. When you accept a counteroffer, often for more money, your original employer now has higher expectations of you than before. In many cases, employers also harbor animosity towards the employee

who they gave a counteroffer to because of the demands they have met to keep you. There is also a lack of trust after someone accepts a counteroffer, which then has to be rebuilt, if it can be reestablished at all.

3. If your coworkers find out about the counteroffer that you have accepted, they can often treat you differently and many times, they become resentful and your working relationships can change.

The only occasions where I have seen a counteroffer situation work out for the employee who chooses to accept a counteroffer, are those where the employee really did NOT want to leave to begin with and felt that they had no other choice. This sometimes happens when a company will tell their employee to go out and get a counteroffer because otherwise they will not be able to give them the increase they deserve.

Again, situations where an employee accepts a counteroffer and it works out are rare occasions, but in a majority of the situations I have come across, most accepted counteroffer situations end poorly with the job seeker ultimately leaving the employer within a few months of accepting the counteroffer. The next time you get a counteroffer, think carefully about why you were intending to leave in the first place and ask yourself if it is worth it long-term to stay.

## FIRST IMPRESSIONS

Making a good first impression is important on any occasion, but one of the most important first impressions you will ever make is the day you start a new job. This is true for both temporary assignments and for full-time positions. I have had people get hired full time on their first day of a temporary assignment because they made such a great first impression, and I have also had people get fired after only a few days in a full-time position because they made a poor first impression. What are a few rules of thumb when it comes to making a good first impression when starting any new job, be it temporary or permanent?

1. Always dress professionally your first day unless otherwise informed by the company or your recruiter. I recommend wearing a suit. It is better to be overdressed than underdressed.

2. Show up at least fifteen minutes early. The worst thing you can do the first day of a new job is to show up late.

3. Be prepared! Find out in advance what you need to know before your first day. For example, find out if there is any paperwork that needs to be completed.

4. Be polite to everyone in the office, from the receptionist to the executives.

5. Listen attentively to everything that is said to you.

6. Take notes if and when necessary regarding your new job duties.

7. Stick to the allotted break time and lunchtime until otherwise informed.

If you do not know what is appropriate when it comes to office etiquette, then do not be afraid to ask! Each company has its own policies and procedures.

## KEEP YOUR NEW JOB—MAKE YOURSELF INDISPENSABLE

It is always good to keep moving up, but the last thing you want is to be dismissed from a new job and have to find another right away all over again—especially if you have followed my advice and found the "dream job" that you truly love.

Here are some simple guidelines for keeping that job you were so excited to get, so that you do not have to start all over again:

1. Whoever you work for, make their life easier.

2. Conduct yourself with impeccable integrity. Do not only what is asked of you, but more importantly, do all of the things you know you should do, but were not asked to.

3. Listen to what is being asked of you, and answer the question that is being asked of you.

4. Always be reliable and on time.

5. Be the type of person who your boss could trust to run things while he or she is out of the office.

6. Always be the one that others go to for help and be helpful at all times.

7. Anticipate the needs of your boss and take initiative.

8. Learn quickly to know your product, know your client and know your services better than everyone else in your office.

9. Always be learning—this includes taking continuing education classes and keeping up with the latest trends by attending conferences or reading articles, journals and books in your industry.

10. Always display a pleasant attitude and be the type of person that others want to be around.

I have talked to people who have lost jobs from such things as smelling too bad at work to watching porn on the job—the fact coming out that the new employee actually *was* a porn star in his spare time! But if you employ some common sense and follow the guidelines above you should be in for a long and successful term at your new job.

## FIVE PHRASES THAT CAN HURT YOUR CAREER

We have looked at some things to do if you want to keep your dream job. Now it is time to take a look at some things to avoid—namely, five phrases that can subtly damage your standing at work. You may have a good reason for wanting to say them, but that just means it is time to rephrase and use your skills at putting a positive spin on something.

1. "I can't." No employer wants to hear that you cannot do something. Rather than saying you cannot or do not have the skills they need, say something like "That is an area I have always wanted to learn more about."

2. "No." Saying "no" to an employer regarding just about any matter is going to get you into trouble with your career. Employers want to hire "YES" people. Always figure out how to make something work rather than reiterate how it cannot work.

3. "I will try my best." There is no try in business, there is only do. You either give something your all and succeed or you give it your all and fail. There is no in between.

4. "I hope it will work out." People who use words like "hope" and "try" are typically people who do not go on to huge success in business. It is important that you commit to an action rather than "hoping" it turns out.

5. "It was not my fault." People who are unwilling to take responsibility for their actions are often seen as victims and/or martyrs and are rarely promoted. Always take responsibility, even if it was not your fault, and then figure out how to make whatever the problem was right.

## CAN YOU NEGOTIATE A RAISE IN THIS ECONOMY?

Asking for more money in a down economy can be very tricky, which is why it is important to strategically plan out how you intend to do so. One of the most common complaints I hear from employers is that they are sick and tired of the sense of entitlement that their staff has. This includes expecting more money. There is an important difference between expecting more money because you feel entitled to it, and approaching your employer to discuss the value you bring to the organization, which in turn leads to a well-earned increase. So what does this mean?

It means that you should avoid going into your boss's office and "demanding" an increase in pay because you are "overworked and underpaid." Instead, you should wait for the opportune time where you have successfully completed a large project, landed a new client and/or saved the company money. Timing is everything! If you go into your boss's office when that person is having a bad day or the company is struggling, you will most definitely be turned down for a raise. Saying that you are struggling financially to your employer is not a good reason for an increase either. To your employer it may sound like you are not good at managing your money. It is also important to make sure you have strong evidence to make a case for why you deserve an increase. Always ask yourself, "Where am I adding value to my organization?"

I would recommend using one of the following opportunities to bring up the subject of a raise:

1. Opportunity: When someone else in your company has been let go and they are not going to replace that person.

This is a great opportunity to show that you are a team player. Offer to pitch in and help cover that person's role. Always start by offering something without asking for anything in return. Then, once you have been assisting with those additional responsibilities for a few months successfully, you can find a good time to broach the subject of increasing your pay to be commensurate with your new duties and responsibilities (and possibly a promotion down the road).

2. Opportunity: You bring in a big new account (or two).

When you are adding a new revenue stream to a company or bringing on numerous new accounts, the company will typically want to make you happy. If you are able to land a big new account or two, this will provide a future opportunity to discuss an increase in compensation. It is important, however, that you wait until you have successfully produced results with that new account for at least three consecutive months or one quarter. This is critical to creating leverage! Bringing in the account is not enough. You have to show that you have been able to successfully manage and grow that account.

3. Opportunity: You came in below budget.

Saving a company money is always a great way to make a case for why a company should offer you an increase in salary. I know that in some cases, you will be penalized if you do not spend the amount you have budgeted for the year, but those are not the situations I am referring to. Overall, most companies are looking for ways to save money. If you save the company 100k over the course of the year, you can then bring that up during your negotiation and use that as evidence for the value you bring to the company and why you deserve an increase.

4. Opportunity: You exceeded your forecasted numbers or billable hour requirement.

Exceeding a goal or quota is one of the easiest ways to negotiate a higher salary. I remember when I first started recruiting and was consistently exceeding my goals by 30%. It was very easy that year to go in and make a case for why I should receive an increase in the percentage of commission that I was receiving because the numbers spoke for me. Typically, the end of the year during your review is a good time to address a potential increase.

5. Opportunity: Producing consistently better work product than your peers/having a great attitude.

I work with a lot of administrative professionals in my staffing business. I find that many of the administrative professionals I work with have a harder time negotiating an increase in salary because their numbers are not linked to billable hours or sales. The best way to negotiate a higher salary as an administrative professional is to work on all of the following:

- Always be on time and offer to pitch in/work overtime when needed.
- Always double- and triple-check your work.
- Offer to do things for your bosses and/or your peers that are not required of you, but that would be appreciated.
- Always have a good, team-player attitude.
- Work on anticipating your boss's needs/don't always wait for someone to give you something to do. Be proactive!

If you focus on those five components as an administrative professional, you will be noticed and rewarded. The administrative professionals who I have seen apply the above five characteristics typically do not even need to ask for a raise, they just receive it!

In summary, remember that actions speak louder than words and timing is everything when it comes to negotiating a higher salary!

## REINVIGORATING A STALE JOB

Initially, getting a job brings a great feeling, but as time passes, sometimes that early thrill can be lost and a job can start to feel stale. Remember that the primary key to finding and keeping a job that fulfills you is to follow your passion.

What is missing for most people when they get stuck in a rut is the fact that they have lost passion for their job. If you are not passionate and excited about what you do, you will begin to feel stagnant and resentful towards your employer. Often it is not the employer's fault; people just lose sight of their goals and what they are committed to in their lives.

The following is what I would recommend to reinvigorate a stale job:

1. Take inventory of your most valuable skills (communication, writing, selling, organizing etc.) and begin to look at what aspects of your job you most enjoy (traveling, planning, working with clients). Look at both the tangible and intangible things, like closeness to home and environment. Begin to explore different ways that you can utilize your most valuable skills in new and innovative ways in the workplace.

2. Look at what is missing in your job—for example, money, challenge, more interaction with customers and so forth—that would make a difference in your current career.

3. Go out and interview at least five people in your life and ask them questions about where you have surprised them, disappointed them and where they feel you could improve. Performing this exercise will assist in giving you a realistic idea of what you are good at and what you need to work on. You can interview coworkers, family members or acquaintances.

4. Once you have accomplished the above steps, formulate a five-year strategy of where you see yourself going and what sort of career path you need to get on. Perhaps your original position inspired you when you first started in it six years ago, but over time your goals have altered and you need to grow in a new direction.

5. When you have identified and created a five-year end goal, you can then strategize by working your way backwards year by year of how you got yourself to your five-year goal. For example, if you knew you wanted to be a VP of Sales five years from now making 150k or more, you would then look at what you were doing at the four-year mark to get yourself to the five-year mark. You would keep working backwards from your five-year goal until you get to where you need to be in the next six months. It is important to start at the five-year mark and work backwards, rather than starting with six months and looking forwards. In doing this, many people will begin

to feel reinspired about their current career or perhaps realize that they need to start moving in a different direction to get to where they want to be in five years.

The bottom line is if you are not passionate about what you do, you will always find yourself dissatisfied with your job.

## IT IS NEVER TOO LATE

*"It is never too late to be what you might have been."*

*George Eliot*

I went out to dinner with an old friend who I had not seen in over a year. I was shocked and amazed when I walked in the door to the restaurant and saw that my friend had lost close to 100 pounds! She was literally half the woman she used to be and was simply glowing. Over dinner, I was so inspired by her new look that I asked her to share her story with me about how she did it and what had sparked such a big change in her.

She said that she had been over 200 pounds for most of her adult life. She explained that she would avoid doctor's appointments because she knew that when she went in to see the doctor he would give her a hard time about her obesity and make her feel humiliated.

Finally, one day she was walking past a mirror in her bedroom and was awestruck by how much she actually weighed. The cost and impact of her obesity finally impacted upon her. That night she made a conscious decision to create being disciplined and to start eating more healthy foods. She began by researching healthy recipes on the Internet. She did not go for a quick fix like gastric bypass or the latest diet pill like so many of us that are looking for immediate gratification. Instead, over the course of many months, she began cooking unique healthy recipes and even bringing them in for others in her office. The first time she went to her doctor's office after she started eating healthier foods her doctor was amazed that she had lost 20 pounds! He said he was impressed, but not to get her hopes up because most people often gain the weight back within a short time.

Her whole life she had told herself, it is too late . . . I am too old . . . I am never going to lose this weight. It just took one honest look at herself in the mirror to see that she needed to make a change. Now, fourteen months later and over 100 pounds lighter, she is a bright new human being with a new lease on life. After years of having felt put down by her doctors and uninspired, she recalled with tears in her eyes the first time her doctor told her how proud he was of her and that not only had she lost over 100 pounds, but she had added at least 10 or more years to her life. Additionally, she had been on numerous medications for her health and is now off of every single one.

She says there are still hard days where she craves sugar and will allow herself a cupcake when she wants one (we passed on dessert that night), but she no longer beats herself up when she has a little sugar. She has realized that everything in moderation is just right and she now appreciates everything she eats!

So why am I sharing this story with you as the final chapter about having your dream job? My friend's story is not just about losing weight, it is about overcoming obstacles and naysayers and negativity in your life and realizing that it is never too late to start living the life you have always wanted.

This is especially true when it comes to your career. I have seen too many people come to my office and complain about how they are too old or too fat or too this or too that to get the job of their dreams. I think that my friend's story is an inspiring one that should be shared and used to motivate others to do what they have been putting off doing for most of their lives.

If my friend can look at herself in the mirror and realize that she does not like what she sees and begin to make small changes that lead to a big difference in her life, then so can you. One small shift in your perspective can permanently alter the outcome of your life and your career.

There is no time left for more excuses about why you would choose to put off having the life you have always wanted. The time is now and the choice is yours to start living the life and working in the position that you have been dreaming of. Start hunting today for your perfect job. I believe that you can earn and achieve it!

# Helpful Links

THE FOLLOWING ARE LINKS TO WEBSITES THAT BENEFIT JOB-SEEKERS by offering resources, additional career advice, and/or job opportunities.

http://www.linkedin.com

http://www.theladders.com

http://www.pinkslipmixers.com

http://www.indeed.com (website that searches all positions posted on the web in your area)

http://inthecalendar.com/ (website that lists all networking events in your area)

http://www.tweetmyjobs.com

http://www.momcorps.com (website for stay at home moms looking to get back into the workplace)

http://www.jobshouts.com

http://www.jobrapido.com

http://www.monster.com

http://www.linkup.com/

http://www.simplyhired.com

http://www.careerbuilder.com

http://www.craigslist.org

http://www.jobing.com

http://www.twitter.com

http://www.twellow.com

http://www.careerjet.com (website which also searches Craigslist postings)

http://www.dice.com

http://www.facebook.com

http://www.elance.com (website that lists freelancing positions)

http://www.e4myjob.com

http://welchwrite.com/career

http://www.jobacle.com

http://jobfox.com/

http://www.showbizjobs.com/

The following website will help you find out salary information in your area.

http://salary.com/

The following are helpful websites for researching a company prior to an interview.

http://www.hoovers.com

http://www.wisi.com

http://www.earningswhispers.com/Default.asp?

http://www.businesswire.com

http://www.thomasnet.com

http://www.wetfeet.com

http://www.zpub.com/sf/arl/

The following are helpful links for writing your resume with sample resumes.

http://www.resume-now.com

http://www.acvtemplate.com

http://office.microsoft.com/en-us/word-help/create-a-resume-HP005189612.aspx

http://jobsearch.about.com/

The following are helpful links for writing cover letters.

http://www.vault.com

http://www.quintcareers.com/cover_letter_samples.html

The following is a link to a helpful cover letter template.

http://www.resume-resource.com/cover-template.html

The following websites offer free training in areas that many companies require testing in.

http://office.microsoft.com/en-us/training/default.aspx

http://www.lynda.com/

https://web.gsc.edu/fs/mhorton/LSEnglish/tutorials/spellingpitfalls.htm

Test your typing skills at:

http://typingtest.com

Take a personality test here to see what job you are best suited for:

http://www.humanmetrics.com/cgi-win/JTypes2.asp

The following are links to workshops that I have participated in and found helpful throughout the years.

http://www.landmarkworldwide.com/

http://www.understandmen.com/

http://www.tm.org/

# Acknowledgments

THIS BOOK WAS A LABOR OF LOVE THAT WOULD NOT HAVE BEEN POSSIBLE without the support of many people, including many of my friends who shared their input throughout the process and helped create the design of the book and the book's title (thanks Ian Ng & Katie Brittingham). I especially want to thank my husband, who encouraged me to follow my dreams and has supported me through thick and thin, from starting my own company over four years ago, to writing this book. I also want to thank my mother, who inspired me to start reading as a little girl and was the first person to read my book and give me hours and hours of helpful feedback as we fine tuned each section.

A special thanks to Adam Gray, a talented animation artist, who created the custom cartoons for this book and to Zsanae Davis, my fabulous photographer who made the book shoot so much fun. I also want to acknowledge my talented PR genius, Richard Berman for helping to get my name out there, and his son Charles, who helped me edit a summation of my blogs into book format. Above all else, I want to thank all of the job seekers and clients with whom I have had the privilege of working with over the past ten years. Without what you have taught me, and the opportunities to grow and learn that you have provided to me with through the various trials and tribulations as well as successes, this book would not have been possible.

Deep thanks to all of my family, friends, and community and professional contacts who are dear to my heart. Each of you is special to me and you have contributed to enriching my life, and encouraging me to follow and live my dreams.

If you have a question
you'd like the author to
answer on her blog, please reach
out to Jennifer K. Hill at
info@stophopingstarthunting.com.